AF801813

African Political, Economic, and Security Issues

Additional books in this series can be found on Nova's website under the Series tab.

Additional E-books in this series can be found on Nova's website under the E-books tab.

Global Political Studies

Additional books in this series can be found on Nova's website under the Series tab.

Additional E-books in this series can be found on Nova's website under the E-books tab.

AFRICAN POLITICAL, ECONOMIC, AND SECURITY ISSUES

U.S. POLITICAL AND TRADE RELATIONS WITH AFRICA

AFRICAN POLITICAL, ECONOMIC, AND SECURITY ISSUES

U.S. POLITICAL AND TRADE RELATIONS WITH AFRICA

GREGORY D. FERRO
EDITOR

Nova Science Publishers, Inc.
New York

Copyright © 2012 by Nova Science Publishers, Inc.

All rights reserved. No part of this book may be reproduced, stored in a retrieval system or transmitted in any form or by any means: electronic, electrostatic, magnetic, tape, mechanical photocopying, recording or otherwise without the written permission of the Publisher.

For permission to use material from this book please contact us:
Telephone 631-231-7269; Fax 631-231-8175
Web Site: http://www.novapublishers.com

NOTICE TO THE READER

The Publisher has taken reasonable care in the preparation of this book, but makes no expressed or implied warranty of any kind and assumes no responsibility for any errors or omissions. No liability is assumed for incidental or consequential damages in connection with or arising out of information contained in this book. The Publisher shall not be liable for any special, consequential, or exemplary damages resulting, in whole or in part, from the readers' use of, or reliance upon, this material. Any parts of this book based on government reports are so indicated and copyright is claimed for those parts to the extent applicable to compilations of such works.

Independent verification should be sought for any data, advice or recommendations contained in this book. In addition, no responsibility is assumed by the publisher for any injury and/or damage to persons or property arising from any methods, products, instructions, ideas or otherwise contained in this publication.

This publication is designed to provide accurate and authoritative information with regard to the subject matter covered herein. It is sold with the clear understanding that the Publisher is not engaged in rendering legal or any other professional services. If legal or any other expert assistance is required, the services of a competent person should be sought. FROM A DECLARATION OF PARTICIPANTS JOINTLY ADOPTED BY A COMMITTEE OF THE AMERICAN BAR ASSOCIATION AND A COMMITTEE OF PUBLISHERS.

Additional color graphics may be available in the e-book version of this book.

Library of Congress Cataloging-in-Publication Data

U.S. political and trade relations with Africa / editor, Gregory D. Ferro.
p. cm.
Includes index.
ISBN 978-1-61209-956-9 (hardcover)
1. United States--Foreign relations--Africa. 2. Africa--Foreign relations--United States. 3. United States--Foreign economic relations--Africa. 4. Africa--Foreign economic relations--United States. I. Ferro, Gregory D. II. Title: US political and trade relations with Africa.
DT38.7.U35 2011
327.7306--dc22
2011007696

Published by Nova Science Publishers, Inc. † New York

CONTENTS

PREFACE

This new book presents and discusses current research in the study of U.S. economic, political and trade relations with Africa. Topics discussed include U.S. trade and investment relationship with Sub-Saharan Africa; U.S. strategic interests and the role of the U.S. military in Africa; current issues and U.S. relations with South Africa and Ghana.

Chapter 1 - Following the end of the apartheid era in South Africa in the early 1990s, the United States sought to increase economic relations with Sub-Saharan Africa. President Clinton instituted several measures that dealt with investment, debt relief, and trade. Congress required the President to develop a trade and development policy for Africa.

The economic challenges facing Africa today are serious. Unlike the period from 1960 to 1973, when economic growth in Sub-Saharan Africa was relatively strong, since 1973 the countries of Sub-Saharan Africa have grown at rates well below other developing countries. There are some signs of improvement, but problems such as HIV/AIDS and the debt burden are constraining African economic growth.

In May 2000, Congress approved a new U.S. trade and investment policy for Sub-Saharan Africa in the African Growth and Opportunity Act. U.S. trade with and investment in Sub-Saharan Africa have comprised only 1%-2% of U.S. totals for the world. AGOA extends preferential treatment to imports from eligible countries that are pursuing market reform measures. Data show that U.S. imports under AGOA are mostly energy products, but imports to date of other products have grown. AGOA mandated that U.S. officials meet regularly with their counterparts in Sub-Saharan Africa, and six of these meetings have been held.

AGOA also directed the President to provide U.S. government technical assistance and trade capacity support to AGOA beneficiary countries. Government agencies that have roles in this effort include the U.S. Agency for International Development, the Assistant U.S. Trade Representative for Africa (established by statute under AGOA), the Overseas Private Investment Corporation, the Export-Import Bank, the U.S. and Foreign Commercial Service, and the Trade and Development Agency. In addition to bilateral programs, the United States is a member of several multilateral institutions that provide trade capacity building.

In AGOA, Congress declared that free-trade agreements should be negotiated, where feasible, with interested Sub-Saharan African countries. Related to this provision, negotiations on a free- trade agreement with the Southern African Customs Union, which includes South Africa and four other countries, began in June 2003, but were suspended in April 2006.

Several topics may be important to the 111th Congress in the oversight of AGOA and in potential legislation amending the act. First, S. 1141 seeks to establish a trade preference program for least-developed countries such as Afghanistan, Bangladesh, and Yemen. Second, an emerging area of concern for Sub-Saharan African countries is growing interest in Congress over reforming trade preference programs by combining existing programs, some of which are due to expire by the end of 2009, into a unified package. Some African leaders have expressed concern that a preference program giving trade benefits similar to those enjoyed by AGOA countries, or creating one trade preference program for all developing countries, would lead to erosion of the preferences granted to African countries under AGOA, and place them in direct competition for U.S. market share and investment with other developing and least-developed countries such as Bangladesh and Cambodia.

Chapter 2 - On February 6, 2007, the Bush Administration announced the creation of a new unified combatant command, U.S. Africa Command or AFRICOM, to promote U.S. national security objectives in Africa and its surrounding waters. Prior to AFRICOM's establishment, U.S. military involvement on the continent was divided among three commands: U.S. European Command (EUCOM), U.S. Central Command (CENTCOM), and U.S. Pacific Command (PACOM). The new command's area of responsibility (AOR) includes all African countries except Egypt. AFRICOM was officially launched as a sub-unified command under EUCOM on October 1, 2007, and became a stand-alone command on October 1, 2008.

In recent years, analysts and U.S. policymakers have noted Africa's growing strategic importance to U.S. interests. Among those interests are the increasing importance of Africa's natural resources, particularly energy resources, and mounting concern over violent extremist activities and other potential threats posed by uncontrolled spaces, such as piracy and illicit trafficking. In addition, there is ongoing concern for Africa's many humanitarian crises, armed conflicts, and more general challenges, such as the devastating effect of HIV/AIDS. In 2006, Congress authorized a feasibility study on the creation of a new command for Africa to consolidate current operations and activities on the continent under one commander. Congress has closely monitored the command since its establishment.

As envisioned by the Department of Defense (DOD), AFRICOM aims promote U.S. strategic objectives by working with African states and regional organizations to help strengthen regional stability and security through improved security capability and military professionalization. If directed by national command authorities, its military operations would aim to deter aggression and respond to crises.

DOD signaled its intention to locate AFRICOM's headquarters on the continent early in the planning process, but such a move is unlikely to take place for several years, if at all. U.S officials are consulting with strategic partners in the region to determine what type of presence on the continent would be most appropriate, and what location, or locations, might be most suitable. The new command will operate from Stuttgart, Germany for the foreseeable future. DOD has stressed that there are no plans to have a significant troop presence on the continent. The East African country of Djibouti, home to the Combined Joint Task Force–Horn of Africa (CJTF-HOA), provides the U.S. military's only enduring infrastructure in Africa.

The 1998 bombing of U.S. embassies in East Africa, and more recent attacks, have highlighted the threat of terrorism to U.S. interests on the continent. Political instability and civil wars have created vast ungoverned spaces, areas in which some experts allege that terrorist groups may train and operate. Instability also heightens human suffering and retards economic development, which may in turn threaten U.S. economic interests. Africa's exports of crude oil to the United States are now roughly equal to those of the Middle East, further emphasizing the continent's strategic importance. This report provides a broad overview of U.S. strategic interests in Africa and the role of U.S. military efforts on the continent as they pertain to the creation of AFRICOM. A discussion of AFRICOM's mission, its coordination with other government agencies, and its basing and manpower requirements is included.

Chapter 3 - Over a decade after the South African majority gained its independence from white minority rule under apartheid, a system of racial segregation, the Republic of South Africa is firmly established as a regional power. With Africa's largest Gross Domestic Product (GDP), a diverse economy, and a government that has played an active role in the promotion of regional peace and stability, South Africa is poised to have a substantial impact on the economic and political future of Africa. The country is twice the size of Texas and has a population of almost 50 million, of which about 80% is African and 10% white. Its political system is regarded as stable, but South Africa faces serious long-term challenges arising from poverty, unemployment, and AIDS. President Thabo Mbeki resigned in September 2008 and was replaced by interim President Kgalema Motlanthe. South Africa's most recent elections were held on April 22, 2009.

The African National Congress (ANC), which led the struggle against apartheid, has dominated the political scene since the end of apartheid and continues to enjoy widespread support in South Africa. The party fell short of retaining its two-thirds majority in the parliament during the 2009 elections, however. Inter-party divisions, which led to Mbeki's resignation in 2008, resulted in the formation of a breakaway party, the Congress of the People (COPE). COPE received 7.4% of the 2009 vote, picking up 30 seats in the 400-seat parliament. The ANC now holds 264 seats, while the main opposition party, the Democratic Alliance (DA), holds 67 seats and gained control of one of the country's nine provinces. Jacob Zuma, elected as head of the ANC in December 2007, weathered a series of corruption charges and was chosen by the ANC-dominated parliament after the 2009 national elections to serve as South Africa's newest President. Motlanthe now serves as Deputy President.

South Africa has the largest HIV/AIDS population in the world, with almost six million South Africans reportedly HIV positive. The former Mbeki Administration's policy on HIV/AIDS was controversial. The country has weathered a series of corruption scandals, and continues to struggle with high crime and unemployment rates. Mounting social tensions related to the competition for jobs, resources, and social services led to an eruption of xenophobic violence against immigrants in mid-2008. The government and the private sector have undertaken a wide variety of construction and infrastructure projects in preparation for the upcoming 2010 soccer World Cup. South Africa has benefitted from steady economic growth in recent years, although economists predict weaker growth prospects for the near future.

South Africa is considered to be one of the United States' two strategic partners on the continent, along with Nigeria. Bilateral relations are cordial, however, the U.S. and South African administrations have expressed differences with respect to the situations in Zimbabwe, Iran, and Iraq, and U.S. officials have articulated frustration with the South African government on positions it took while serving on the United Nations Security Council. This report will be updated as events warrant.

Chapter 4 - This report provides information on current developments in Ghana and Ghana's relations with the United States, which are close. It describes the purpose of President Barack Obama's forthcoming trip to Ghana, which will focus on issues of good governance and socio-economic and political development, and characterizes the current state of play in bilateral relations. It also summarizes the policy agenda of Ghana's president, John Atta Mills, who won office by a narrow margin in elections in late 2008. The dynamics of that election are described in the report, as are recent policy-centered developments, economic challenges and performance, and socio-economic prospects. Ghana's international relations and bilateral development cooperation with the United States are also covered in the report.

Versions of these chapters were also published in *Current Politics and Economics of Africa,* Volume 3, Numbers 1-4, edited by Frank Columbus, published by Nova Science Publishers, Inc. They were submitted for appropriate modifications in an effort to encourage wider dissemination of research.

In: U.S. Political and Trade Relations with Africa ISBN 978-1-61209-956-9
Editor: Gregory D. Ferro © 2012 Nova Science Publishers, Inc.

Chapter 1

U.S. TRADE AND INVESTMENT RELATIONSHIP WITH SUB-SAHARAN AFRICA: THE AFRICAN GROWTH AND OPPORTUNITY ACT*

Vivian C. Jones

ABSTRACT

Following the end of the apartheid era in South Africa in the early 1990s, the United States sought to increase economic relations with Sub-Saharan Africa. President Clinton instituted several measures that dealt with investment, debt relief, and trade. Congress required the President to develop a trade and development policy for Africa.

The economic challenges facing Africa today are serious. Unlike the period from 1960 to 1973, when economic growth in Sub-Saharan Africa was relatively strong, since 1973 the countries of Sub-Saharan Africa have grown at rates well below other developing countries. There are some signs of improvement, but problems such as HIV/AIDS and the debt burden are constraining African economic growth.

In May 2000, Congress approved a new U.S. trade and investment policy for Sub-Saharan Africa in the African Growth and

---

*This is an edited, reformatted and augmented version of CRS Report RL31772, dated July 24, 2009.

Opportunity Act (AGOA; Title I, P.L. 106-200). U.S. trade with and investment in Sub-Saharan Africa have comprised only 1%-2% of U.S. totals for the world. AGOA extends preferential treatment to imports from eligible countries that are pursuing market reform measures. Data show that U.S. imports under AGOA are mostly energy products, but imports to date of other products have grown. AGOA mandated that U.S. officials meet regularly with their counterparts in Sub-Saharan Africa, and six of these meetings have been held.

AGOA also directed the President to provide U.S. government technical assistance and trade capacity support to AGOA beneficiary countries. Government agencies that have roles in this effort include the U.S. Agency for International Development, the Assistant U.S. Trade Representative for Africa (established by statute under AGOA), the Overseas Private Investment Corporation, the Export-Import Bank, the U.S. and Foreign Commercial Service, and the Trade and Development Agency. In addition to bilateral programs, the United States is a member of several multilateral institutions that provide trade capacity building.

In AGOA, Congress declared that free-trade agreements should be negotiated, where feasible, with interested Sub-Saharan African countries. Related to this provision, negotiations on a free- trade agreement with the Southern African Customs Union, which includes South Africa and four other countries, began in June 2003, but were suspended in April 2006.

Several topics may be important to the 111th Congress in the oversight of AGOA and in potential legislation amending the act. First, S. 1141 (Feinstein, introduced May 21, 2009, the TRADE Act of 2009) seeks to establish a trade preference program for least-developed countries such as Afghanistan, Bangladesh, and Yemen. Second, an emerging area of concern for Sub-Saharan African countries is growing interest in Congress over reforming trade preference programs by combining existing programs, some of which are due to expire by the end of 2009, into a unified package. Some African leaders have expressed concern that a preference program giving trade benefits similar to those enjoyed by AGOA countries, or creating one trade preference program for all developing countries, would lead to erosion of the preferences granted to African countries under AGOA, and place them in direct competition for U.S. market share and investment with other developing and least-developed countries such as Bangladesh and Cambodia.

INTRODUCTION

All of us share a common vision for the future of Africa. We look to the day when prosperity for Africa is built through trade and markets.

—President George W. Bush to delegates at the African Growth and Opportunity Forum in Mauritius, January 15, 2003.

Source: Map resources. Adapted by CRS (6/21/2004).

Figure 1. Africa.

As reflected in the above statement by President Bush, a key element in U.S. policy toward Africa is the potential benefit from improved commerce between the two regions. This interest in increasing bilateral commerce began after the end of the apartheid era in South Africa in the early 1990s. In 1993, Congress approved the end of anti-apartheid restrictions, and later that year Commerce Secretary Ron Brown led a business delegation to South Africa.

With the end of apartheid, President Clinton instituted numerous measures to help the region and increase U.S. trade and investment there. In 1994, he announced a $600 million aid and investment package for South Africa. In 1997, he proposed the Partnership for Economic Growth and Opportunity in Africa, which offered different levels of economic benefits to countries in sub-Saharan Africa (SSA), depending on their economic reform measures.

At the same time, Congress was developing legislation that sought to improve U.S.-Africa trade relations. In the 1994 legislation to implement the Uruguay Round multilateral trade agreements (P.L. 103-465), Congress directed the Administration to develop and implement a comprehensive trade and development policy for the countries of Africa. Disappointed with the Administration's first report under this provision, some Members developed legislation to authorize a new trade and investment policy for sub-Saharan Africa. In May 2000, Congress approved such legislation in the African Growth and Opportunity Act (AGOA; Title I, P.L. 106-200). AGOA offers trade preferences and other economic benefits to countries in SSA that meet certain criteria, including progress towards a market economy, respect for the rule of law, and human and worker rights.

Both the executive and legislative branches continue to consider ways in which to improve trade relations between the United States and SSA. In 2002, the Congress amended AGOA to further increase market access for products from SSA [1]. The Administration began free-trade negotiations with the South African Customs Union (Botswana, Namibia, Lesotho, South Africa, and Swaziland) in June 2003. In 2004 Congress passed legislation further amending AGOA, extending its benefits beyond the original deadline and clarifying certain provisions. This legislation also included directives to the President on investment initiatives and technical assistance. Congress passed legislation in December 2006 which further amends AGOA, to extend certain provisions concerning textile and apparel imports to 2012 [2].

This report presents perspectives on African economic trends and provides an overview of U.S. trade and investment flows with SSA. It discusses the provisions of AGOA and the changes that have occurred since its enactment. It concludes with a brief discussion of issues of congressional interest.

PERSPECTIVES ON THE SUB-SAHARAN AFRICAN ECONOMY

Historical Perspectives

The historical pattern of contemporary Africa's economic growth provides insights to help understand Africa's current economic situation and policy options. Between 1960 and 1973, which is the period immediately following independence in most African countries, economic growth was reasonably strong in much of Sub-Saharan Africa (SSA). The subsequent two decades were, however, a period of stagnation or decline for most countries [3]. The causes of Africa's slow and stagnant economic growth have been a source of debate among development economists. Analysts have cited poor governance, political instability, geographic features, and historical conditions such as colonialism as different reasons for Africa's economic malaise. Whatever the underlying cause, Africa's slow growth and stagnation have been attributed to slow accumulation of both human and physical capital, dependence on single commodity exports, low productivity growth and pressures from high population growth rates [4].

Most African countries experienced a sharp decline in their growth trends at some point between 1973 and 1980, followed by persistent stagnation until the early 1990s. Average SSA per-capita GDP reached its minimum point in the mid 1990s, and still had not recovered to 1970s levels in 2005 [5]. High economic growth volatility is a common feature in SSA countries' historical trends. A recent World Bank study finds that SSA has experienced more growth volatility than other regions, resulting in dampened investments and obscuring periods of good performance for some countries. This volatility has been caused by conflict, poor governance, and fluctuating world commodity prices. The authors of the study contend that reducing volatility is at least as important as promoting growth [6]. Recent data demonstrate that many African countries have made a modest recovery since about 1994, but the growth rates for the remainder of the 1 990s tended to remain far below the first post-colonial phase [7]. For the four decades as a whole, SSA's average per capita income growth of 0.9 % lagged behind that of other developing countries by 1.5% and approximately 3% below that of the high-performing African economies (Botswana and Mauritius) [8].

Individual African countries have shown widely divergent economic growth performance. A recent study found that in a group of 36 African countries, 22 countries exhibited reasonably robust growth before the long period of stagnation. The remaining 14 either experienced sharp growth fluctuations or showed persistent stagnation at growth rates below 1.5% throughout the last three decades. In this study, the high growth rates achieved by Botswana and Mauritius stand out [9].

The consequence of the long period of stagnation for a large number of African economies, combined with high population growth rates, is that little or no progress has been made in raising the standards of living in these countries. Many African countries have experienced a decrease in the standard of living.10 Between 1960 and 1994, out of 35 SSA countries for which comparable data exist, 16 suffered at least 20% loss in income per capita measured in 1985 constant U.S. dollars. Most of the losses were registered after 1975 [11]. In contrast to SSA, developed countries have sustained a remarkably steady per capita growth of approximately 2% for about 100 years, and some newly industrializing countries have maintained income growth rates above 3% for nearly three decades, thus enabling them to gain significant ground on the industrialized countries [12].

Current Perspectives

According to the World Bank, Sub-Saharan Africa's resilient economic growth performance over the past decade suggests that it may have achieved a milestone in its quest for sustained growth. SSA's economic performance from 1995 to 2005 "reverses the collapses in 1975-1985 and the stagnations in 1985-1995" [13]. Its growth has averaged 4.0% between 2000 and 2005, compared with less than 1% during the early 1990s. In 2006, GDP expanded by 5.6 % in SSA, followed by 6.2 % in 2007, and 5.2 % in 2008. During that time period, analysts also considered the growth trends as less volatile and more evenly distributed among African countries than in the past. Twenty-two countries (out of a total 48 Sub-Saharan African countries) had average growth rates of 4% or greater during the past five years, as compared with only four countries in the first half of the 1990s. In 2006, half of the SSA countries experienced growth of 5% or more. This improved economic performance may reflect many factors, including better governance, increased trade flows, strong commodity prices, rising aid flows, and debt forgiveness [14].

Although the global financial crisis did not initially hit Africa directly, the effects of the global economic downturn are now beginning to be felt. IHS Global Insight projects that Sub-Saharan Africa's real GDP will grow only

0.2% in 2009, down from 5.2% in 2008. Real GDP growth in the region is projected to grow by 2.2% in 2010, and 4.0% in 2011. In contrast, however, the growth rate for the world in 2009 is forecasted to contract to a negative 2.4%, with modest economic recovery expected in 2010 (1.7%) and 2011 (2.2%) [15].

Foreign direct investment in the region has been strong in recent years. According to the Economist Intelligence Unit, inward direct investment flows amounted to $12 billion in 2005, $14 billion in 2006, $18 billion in 2007 and $20 billion in 2008 [16]. However, as the results of the global economic downturn continue to be felt in Sub-Saharan Africa and other regions, investment is expected to decline to $4 billion in 2009, and then increase once again to $6 million in 2010, and $11 billion in 2011 [17].

Investment and Growth Challenges

Despite the region's improved economic performance, the economic challenges facing Africa remain enormous. African countries are vulnerable to volatile weather conditions, commodity price fluctuations, poor road and other infrastructure conditions, and political events in parts of the continent.

Much of Sub-Saharan Africa's trade with the world is largely still reliant on primary product exports, such as oil and other mineral fuels (68% of its exports to the world by value in 2008); ores, slag and ash (about 14% by value); and precious stones (about 4% by value) [18]. As a result, many Sub-Saharan African countries continue to be vulnerable—as do many developing countries and regions—to the rise and fall of international commodity prices. Correspondingly, the global slump in oil prices, combined with price declines and decreased demand for other primary products due to the world economic downturn, have dealt a severe blow to the region.

HIV/AIDS [19]

The HIV/AIDS pandemic is also straining African economies and threatens to curtail future economic growth. The prevalence of HIV/AIDS in SSA was estimated at 6.1% in late 2005, compared with 1.1% worldwide. By 2007, the incidence decreased to 5%, compared to 0.8% worldwide.20 Nine countries in southern Africa had incidence rates of over 10 percent. Botswana, long considered one of the region's most successful economies, had an incidence rate of 25.9% as of 2006. Only Swaziland had a higher HIV/AIDS incidence rate than Botswana in 2006, at 25.9%. The pandemic not only diverts resources from investments in productive resources and social services to care for the sick and dying, but it also erodes human capital by striking some of the most productive members of society: skilled workers, teachers, and professionals [21].

Debt

The debt burden carried by SSA countries has been identified as a drag on the economies of the region. At the end of 2007, the states of SSA owed foreign creditors a total of $195.1 billion.22 While SSA's debt is comparable to other regions in terms of absolute amount, per capita share ($244 per head), or debt service as percentage of export earnings (5.0% in 2007), its debt burden has been considered onerous because of its high ratio of debt to income.23 Africa's total debt was equal to 66% of its income in 2002. As of late 2007, Africa's total debt stood at about 20% of its income.24 Declines in SSA's external debt were due to comprehensive debt relief initiatives including the Heavily Indebted Poor Countries Initiative (HIPC), the Multilateral Debt Relief Initiative (MDRI), and the Paris Club agreement with Nigeria [25].

U.S.-Africa Trade and Investment Trends

U.S. Trade with Sub-Saharan Africa

The United States conducts a small share of its total trade with Sub-Saharan Africa. In 2008, the United States exported $18 billion to Sub-Saharan Africa, or 1.6% of total U.S. global exports of $1,070 billion. The United States imported $86.1 billion from the region, or 4.1% of its total imports of $2,090 billion. Total trade (exports plus imports) between the United States and Sub- Saharan Africa more than quadrupled between 1990 and 2007, from $17 billion to $81 billion. However, U.S. trade with Sub-Saharan Africa as a share of total U.S. trade did not increase as dramatically from 1990 to 2007, from 1.9 % in 1990 to 2.7% in 2007.

Most U.S. trade with Sub-Saharan Africa is with a small number of countries. Seventy percent of U.S. imports from the region were from three SSA countries in 2008: Nigeria (44%), Angola (22%), and South Africa (12%). Exports were similarly concentrated, with three countries receiving 68%: South Africa (34%), Nigeria (22%), and Angola (12%). The remaining countries each accounted for less than 6% of U.S. exports to the region. (See Figure 3).

Natural resources dominate U.S. imports from Sub-Saharan Africa. Nearly all U.S. imports from the region in 2008 were energy products (83 percent), which were almost exclusively petroleum, or minerals and metals (see Figure 4). Nigeria was the largest African and fifth-largest overall oil supplier to the United States. It supplied 53% of U.S. petroleum imports from the region, which accounted for 8% of total global U.S. oil imports. Angola supplied another 26% of U.S. petroleum from the region, and Congo(ROC) supplied 7%.

Table 1. U.S. Trade with Sub-Saharan Africa Domestic Exports, FAS value; Imports for Consumption, Customs Value; Actual U.S. dollars

Trade Flow	2007	2008	Jan. –May 2008	Jan. –May 2009
U.S. Exports	13,860,275,557	18,007,646,662	6,482,230,963	5,852,442,459
U.S. Imports	66,888,558,420	86,082,041,604	28,100,634,572	12,126,201,385
U.S. Total Trade	80,748,833,977	104,089,688,266	34,582,865,535	17,978,643,844
(Imports +Exports)				

Source: U.S. International Trade Commission Trade Dataweb, http://dataweb.usitc .gov.

Other petroleum exporters from the region included Chad, Gabon, and Equatorial Guinea, supplying between 3 and 5% of U.S. oil imports from Africa.

The most important U.S. mineral/metal imports from Africa were platinum, followed by diamonds. U.S. exports to Sub-Saharan Africa were more diverse. Machinery and parts was the leading export sector in 2008 (22% of U.S. exports to the region), followed by transportation equipment (17%), cereals (8%), mineral fuels (8%), aircraft and parts (7%), and electrical machinery (6%) (see Figure 5).

In terms of Sub-Saharan Africa's trade with the world, the European Union was SSA's largest export trading partner in 2008 ($99 billion), followed by the United States ($85.7 billion), China ($43.6 billion), India ($19.3 billion), Japan ($13.5 billion), and Brazil ($10.3 billion).

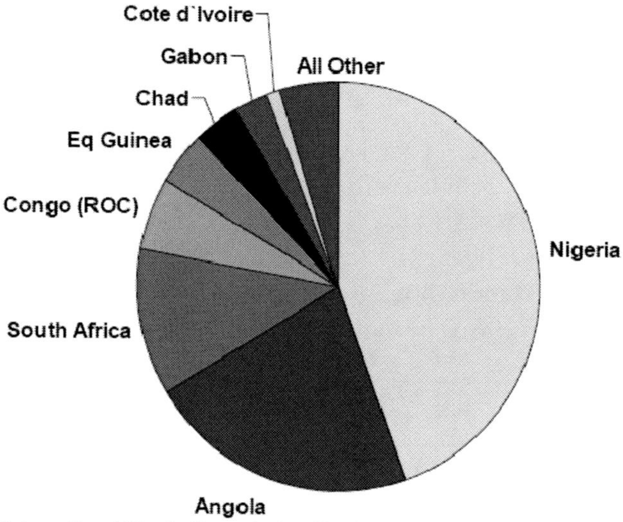

Source: U.S. International Trade Commission Trade Dataweb, http://www.usitc.gov.

Figure 2. U.S. Imports from Sub-Saharan Africa, 2008.

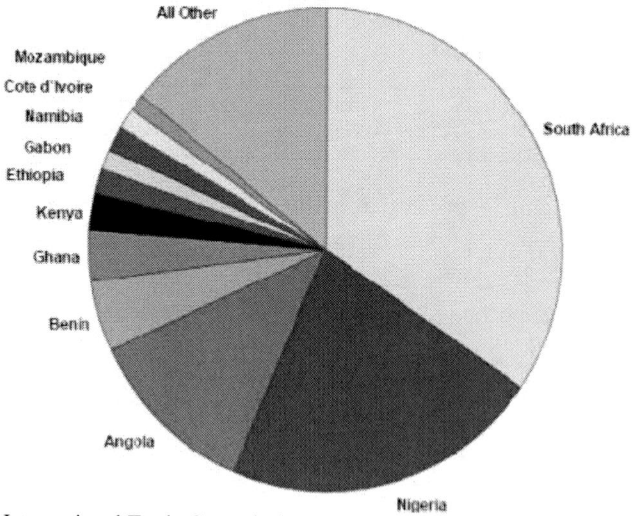

Source: U.S. International Trade Commission Trade Dataweb, http://dataweb.usitc.gov.

Figure 3. U.S. Exports to Sub-Saharan Africa, 2008.

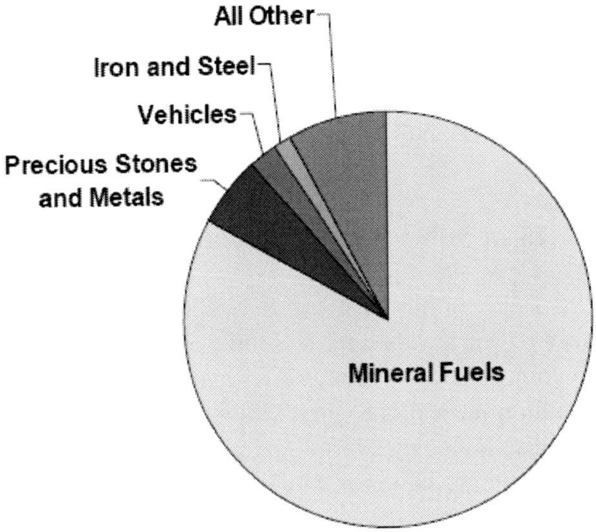

Source: U.S. International Trade Commission Trade Dataweb, http://www.usitc.gov.

Figure 4. U.S. Imports from Sub-Saharan Africa by Product Category, 2008.

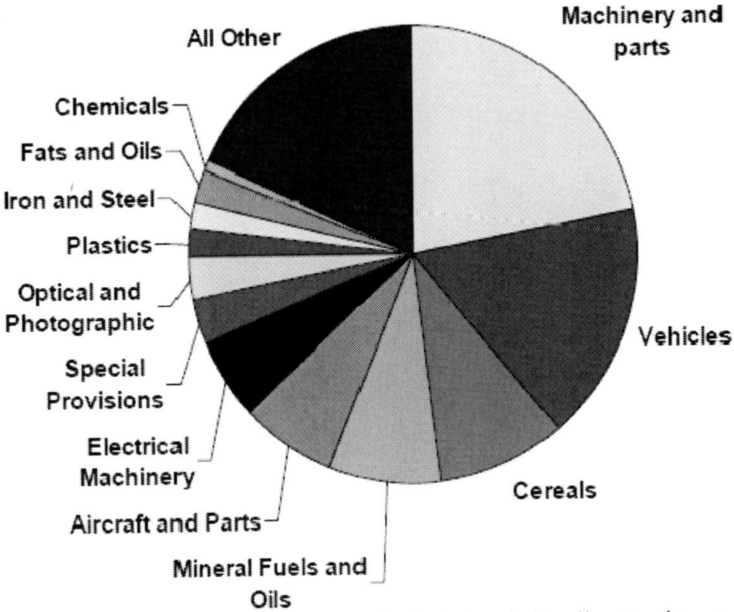

Source: U.S. International Trade Commission Trade Dataweb, http://www.usitc.gov.

Figure 5. U.S. Exports to Sub-Saharan Africa by Product Category, 2008.

The European Union was also Sub-Saharan Africa's leading import trading partner ($85.3 billion), followed by China ($34.5 billion), the United States ($18.2 billion), India ($11.9 billion), South Korea ($9.3 billion), and Japan ($9.3 billion) [26].

U.S. Investment in Sub-Saharan Africa

Similar to trade, U.S. investment in Sub-Saharan Africa represents a very small percentage of worldwide total U.S. investment. At year-end 2008, total U.S. direct investment in Sub-Saharan Africa was $36.6 billion, or about 1% of the $3,162 billion in total U.S. direct investment abroad [27]. U.S. capital outflows to Africa (including North Africa) increased steadily from $20.4 billion in 2004, to $22.8 billion in 2005, to $28.2 billion in 2006, to $32.6 billion in 2007, and $36.6 billion in 2008. 28 U.S. investment in Africa is heavily toward natural resources: In 2008, 77% of total U.S. investment in Africa (including Egypt) was in the mining sector (includes petroleum extraction), compared to 18% in holding companies, 10% in other manufacturing, 3% in primary and fabricated metals, and 3% in wholesale trade. About 9% of total U.S. investment in the mining sector worldwide is in Africa [29].

In 2008, South Africa led the SSA region in U.S. investment flows to Africa, with 13.4% (of the total $36.6 billion invested in Africa in 2008), followed by Nigeria (9.26%), Equatorial Guinea (8.1%), Mauritius, (6.6%), and Angola (5.8%) [30].

AGOA: Legislation

Action in 111th Congress

Some in Congress have proposed reforming trade preference programs such as the Generalized System of Preferences (GSP) and the Andean Trade and Partnership Act (ATPA), both of which expire by the end of 2009. In particular, a group of business and NGO groups have proposed providing duty-free, quota-free (DFQF) U.S. market access to all least-developed countries (LDCs) [31]. Congressman Jim McDermott is reportedly planning to introduce a bill in the 111th Congress seeking to reform these programs in a way that would grant DFQF access to designated LDCs and Sub-Saharan

African countries, similar to legislation (H.R. 3905 of the 110th Congress) that he introduced in the previous Congress [32] S. 1141 (Feinstein), the TRADE Act of 2009, seeks to create a trade preference program for designated least-developed countries, including Afghanistan, Bangladesh, and Cambodia, in a similar model to AGOA, and with similar trade benefits.

Many Sub-Saharan African countries have expressed concern that an such an approach to trade preference reform could place them in direct competition for U.S. market share with countries like Bangladesh and Cambodia, thus diluting the value of the preferential treatment that they currently receive through the AGOA preference. Some African business interests are also reportedly working to limit the textile and apparel benefit provisions in a bill that would designate Reconstruction Opportunity Zones in Afghanistan and Pakistan on the basis that the proposed benefits would harm the exports of SSA countries and set a bad precedent for legislation to reform existing preference programs [33].

Current Provisions and Amendments

In May 2000, Congress approved legislation, the African Growth and Opportunity Act (AGOA; Title I, Trade and Development Act of 2000; P.L. 106-200), to assist the economies of Sub-Saharan Africa and to improve economic relations between the United States and the region. This section examines the major provisions of AGOA, related legislative initiatives, and other developments since enactment.

Beneficiary Countries and Trade Benefits

Subtitle A of AGOA authorized the President to designate Sub-Saharan African countries as beneficiary countries eligible to receive duty-free treatment for certain articles that are the growth, product, or manufacture of that country. It directed that in designating a beneficiary country, the President must determine that the country (1) has established, or is making continual progress toward establishing a market-based economy and is taking other designated actions; (2) does not engage in activities that undermine U.S. national security and foreign policy interests; and (3) does not engage in gross violations of internationally recognized human rights or provide support for international terrorism.

Subtitle B of AGOA describes trade-related benefits that are available to AGOA-eligible countries. Among these benefits is preferential duty-free treatment for certain articles under the U.S. Generalized System of Preferences (GSP). The GSP program is a unilateral trade preference regime that allows certain products from designated developing countries to enter the United States duty-free. Certain categories of articles (see box) are identified in statute as ineligible for this duty-free treatment, because they are "import sensitive." AGOA provides that the President can grant GSP duty-free treatment to all of these articles except one category (see box, textiles and apparel). First, however, after receiving advice from the International Trade Commission, the President must determine that an article is not import-sensitive in the context of imports from AGOA beneficiaries. These additional articles qualifying for GSP duty-free treatment have to be the growth, product, or manufacture of an AGOA beneficiary country, and they must meet the GSP rules of origin as amended under AGOA. AGOA beneficiaries are exempt from certain limits under the GSP program on allowable duty-free imports ("competitive need limitation") [34].

Import-sensitive" articles that are ineligible for preferences under GSP:

1. Textile and apparel articles which were not eligible articles for purposes of this subchapter on January 1, 1994, as this subchapter was in effect on such date.
2. Watches, except those watches entered after June 30, 1989, that the President specifically determines, after public notice and comment, will not cause material injury to watch or watch band, strap, or bracelet manufacturing and assembly operations in the United States or the United States insular possessions.
3. Import-sensitive electronic articles.
4. Footwear, handbags, luggage, flat goods, work gloves, and leather wearing apparel which were not eligible articles for purposes of this subchapter on January 1, 1995, as this subchapter was in effect on such date.
5. Import-sensitive semi-manufactured and manufactured glass products.
6. Any other articles which the President determines to be import-sensitive in the context of the Generalized System of Preferences.

Textiles and Apparel

AGOA also allows duty-free and quota-free treatment for textiles and apparel under any of the following conditions:

- Apparel must be assembled in one or more AGOA beneficiary countries from U.S. fabric that was made from U.S. yarns and cut in the United States;
- Apparel must be assembled in one or more AGOA beneficiary countries from U.S. fabric that was made from U.S. yarns. The apparel must be cut in an AGOA country and assembled using U.S. thread; or
- Apparel must be assembled in one or more AGOA beneficiary countries from fabric made in one or more AGOA beneficiary countries from yarn made in the United States or an AGOA beneficiary country. These imports were limited under AGOA to 1.5% of all U.S. imports (in aggregate square meter equivalents) in FY2001, increasing to 3.5% over eight years. (This limit was later amended; see "Amendments to AGOA" below.)
- For an apparel product of a less developed AGOA beneficiary country (defined as having a per capita gross national product less than $1,500 in 1998 as measured by the World Bank), that product qualifies for duty-free and quota-free treatment through September 30, 2004 (this deadline was later extended to 2007 and then 2012; see "Amendments to AGOA" below), regardless of the country of origin of the fabric. The square meter equivalents cap on products under this category is 3.5% of all U.S. imports.

To receive the duty-free and quota-free treatment for textile and apparel products as described above, beneficiary countries must adopt an efficient visa system to prevent unlawful transshipment. They also must work with the U.S. Customs Service to report exports and prevent illegal trade. AGOA provided that the Secretary of Commerce must monitor for surges in imports, with the possible withdrawal of duty-free treatment if imports surge beyond a certain level.

Developments Following Enactment of AGOA

AGOA was enacted on May 18, 2000. On October 2, 2000, President Clinton recognized the first AGOA beneficiary countries. He identified 34 out of the 48 Sub-Saharan African countries as eligible for AGOA benefits. On December 21, 2000, he granted GSP duty-free treatment to more than 1,800 items from AGOA-eligible countries. These items were selected after public review, advice from the International Trade Commission, and interagency review and recommendation. (These 1,800 items are in addition to about 4,600 items already duty-free under GSP.)

During 2001, the Administration declared that 12 AGOA countries had met the additional requirements for duty-free and quota-free treatment for apparel and textiles. Ten of the 12 countries qualified for the provisions for less-developed countries (LDCs) (see the fourth bullet on the preceding page). Early in 2001, in response to interim regulations that the U.S. Customs Service had issued in October 2000 (65 Fed. Reg. 59,668), some legislators protested that the interim regulations denied duty-free benefits for knit-to-shape articles, contrary to what they said was the intent of the act [35].

AGOA requires that the President monitor and report annually on the progress of each country in meeting the terms for AGOA eligibility. Under this requirement, President Bush has made, at the end of each year, annual designations of the countries eligible for AGOA benefits for the following year. The last such designation was in June 2007, when President Bush designated Mauritania as eligible for AGOA benefits.

Amendments to AGOA

Congress passed legislation to amend AGOA four times since its initial passage. In 2002, Congress amended AGOA for the first time through the Trade Act of 2002 (P.L. 107-2 10). An important change pertained to the cap that AGOA had set on imports of apparel assembled in an AGOA country from fabric made in an AGOA country (see the third bullet under Textiles and Apparel above). The Trade Act of 2002 doubled this cap, increasing it to 7% in FY2008. The act, however, left the cap unchanged at 3.5% under the special rule for lesser-developed countries. The act also allowed Namibia and Botswana to qualify for the special rule for lesser-developed countries, even though their per capita incomes exceed the limit set under AGOA.

The Trade Act of 2002 specifically extended AGOA benefits to knit-to-shape articles and to garments cut in both the United States and an AGOA beneficiary country ("hybrid cutting"). It also made a correction to extend AGOA benefits to merino wool sweaters knit in AGOA beneficiary countries.

The Trade Act included other related provisions. It stated that U.S. workers could be found eligible for trade adjustment assistance, if U.S. production shifted to an AGOA beneficiary country and other conditions were met [36]. It authorized $9.5 million to the Customs Service for textile transshipment enforcement, and specified that two permanent positions be assigned to South Africa for AGOA enforcement and additional travel funds be allocated for verification in Sub-Saharan Africa. It also required that $1.31

7 million of the Customs Service budget be spent on programs to help Sub-Saharan African countries develop visa and anti-transshipment systems.

In July 2004, Congress amended AGOA further through the AGOA Acceleration Act of 2004 (P.L. 108-274). This legislation extended the deadline for AGOA benefits to 2015, and it also extended the special rule for LDCs from September 2004 to September 2007. It further stipulated that the cap on the volume of allowable U.S. apparel imports under this rule would be decreased starting in the year beginning September 2004, with a major reduction in the year beginning October 2006 (from 2.9% to 1.6%). The rationale behind this change was to encourage fabric production and vertical integration of the apparel industry in Africa. For apparel imports meeting the yarn forward rules of origin, the cap is to remain at 7% until the expiration of the benefits in 2015. The legislation also clarified certain apparel rules of origin to reflect the intent of Congress.

Apparel articles containing fabric from both the United States and AGOA beneficiary countries were specifically allowed, as were otherwise eligible apparel articles containing cuffs, collars, and other similar components that did not meet the strict rules of origin. There was also clarification that ethnic printed fabric would qualify for duty-free treatment, as long as the fabric met certain standards regarding its size, form, and design characteristics. In addition, apparel articles containing fabrics and yarns recognized in the North American Free Trade Agreement (NAFTA) as being in short supply in the United States were declared as eligible for duty-free treatment, regardless of the source of such fabric and yarns. The legislation also increased the maximum allowable content of non-regional or non-U.S. fibers or yarns in AGOA eligible apparel imports, otherwise known as the de minimis rule, from 7% to 10%.

The AGOA Acceleration Act included a number of directives for the President. One such directive was to provide agricultural technical assistance by assigning U.S. personnel to at least 10 AGOA beneficiary countries, to help exporters meet U.S. technical standards for agricultural imports. Another directed the President to develop policies to encourage investment in agriculture and agricultural processing, as well as investment in infrastructure projects aimed at improving transportation and communication links both within Africa and between Africa and the United States. There was also a directive to foster improved relationships between African and U.S. customs and transportation authorities. An additional directive was to encourage technical assistance and infrastructure projects to assist in the development of the ecotourism industry in Sub-Saharan Africa. Finally, another directed the

President to conduct a study on each beneficiary country, identifying potential sectors for growth, barriers to such growth, and how U.S. technical assistance can assist each country in overcoming these barriers.

In December 2004, the Miscellaneous Trade and Technical Corrections Act of 2004 (P.L. 108- 429) was passed, which contained a technical correction to the AGOA Acceleration Act. The legislation also allowed Mauritius to qualify for the special rule for LDCs for the one year beginning October 1, 2004, with a cap of 5% of total eligible imports under this rule.

Table 2. Country Status under AGOA (as of January 1, 2009)

Status	Countries
Not Designated as Eligible (8 countries)	Central African Republic; Côte d'Ivoire; Equatorial Guinea; Eritrea; Mauritania; Somalia; Sudan; Zimbabwe.
AGOA Eligible Only, Not Eligible under Apparel Provision (13 countries)	Angola; Burundi; Comoros; Republic of the Congo; Democratic Republic of the Congo; Djibouti; Gabon; Guinea; Guinea-Bissau; Liberia; Sao Tome and Principe; Seychelles; Togo.
AGOA Eligible, Eligible for Apparel Provision, Special Rule Does Not Apply (1 country)	South Africa
AGOA Eligible, Eligible under Apparel Provision, and Special Rule Applies (26 countries)	Benin; Botswana; Burkina Faso; Cameroon; Cape Verde; Chad; Ethiopia; The Gambia; Ghana; Kenya; Lesotho; Madagascar; Malawi; Mali; Mauritius; Mozambique; Namibia; Niger; Nigeria; Rwanda; Senegal; Sierra Leone; Swaziland; Tanzania; Uganda; Zambia

Source: AGOA website maintained by the U.S. Department of Commerce and USTR at http://www.agoa.gov.

Congress passed the Africa Investment Incentive Act of 2006 in December 2006 (Title VI of P.L. 109-432). This act extends the special rule for LDCs which allows textiles and apparel quota- and duty-free access to the U.S. market regardless of the source of materials used, as long as assembly takes place within an AGOA-eligible LDC. The special rule for LDCs would have expired in 2007, but this act extends it to 2012 and increases the cap on square meter equivalents under this rule back to the initial level of 3.5%. This act also contains an "abundant supply" provision stipulating that if a certain fabric is determined by the U.S. International Trade Commission to be available in commercial quantities in AGOA beneficiary countries, then the special rule will no longer apply to apparel and textiles containing that particular fabric.

Current Beneficiaries

At present, 40 Sub-Saharan African countries are designated as AGOA-eligible. Of those countries, 26 have met the additional requirements to receive duty-free treatment for their textile and apparel products, and of those, 25 qualify for the special rule for lesser-developed countries (all but South Africa). See Table 2 for a list of Sub-Saharan African countries and their status under AGOA.

AGOA Trade Trends

In 2007, over 98% of U.S. imports from AGOA-eligible countries entered the United States duty- free, either under the AGOA preference or under most-favored-nation (MFN) tariff rates [37].

The value of U.S. total trade with Sub-Saharan Africa increased by about 29% between 2007 and 2008. After at least three years of continuous growth, however, the value of Sub-Saharan Africa's exports to the United States decreased in value by about 57% in the first five months of 2009, in comparison to the same time period in 2008. The value of U.S. exports to the SSA region in 2008 increased by about 29%, from $13.9 billion in 2007, to $18 billion in 2008. In the first six months of 2009, U.S. exports in value terms decreased about 9%, from $6.5 billion in 2008 to $5.9 billion in 2009.

In 2008, oil and mineral fuels accounted for about 83% of all U.S. imports from Sub-Saharan Africa, and 94% of all U.S. imports under the African Growth and Opportunity Act (AGOA).38 U.S. petroleum imports from SSA in the first part of 2009 in volume terms did not decrease as dramatically as they did by value. For example, U.S. imports to the United States in Harmonized Tariff Schedule (HTS) subheading 2709.00.20 (petroleum oils testing 25 degrees API or more) decreased only 23% by volume, and imports in HTS subheading 2709.00.10 (petroleum oils testing under 25 degrees API) actually increased by almost 9% in volume terms. Since these are the top two products that the United States imports from the region, the rapid decline of the value of U.S. imports can be primarily attributed to the decline in oil prices in the latter part of 2008 and the first part of 2009. However, decreases in U.S. and global consumption are likely to continue to have a negative effect on most exports from the region [39].

United States-Sub-Saharan Africa Trade and Economic Cooperation Forum

Under AGOA, the President was required to establish within a year of enactment, after consultation with Congress and the other governments concerned, a United States- Sub-Saharan Africa Trade and Economic Cooperation Forum (hereinafter referred to as the Forum).

Table 3. Leading U.S. Imports from Sub-Saharan Africa U.S. Imports for Consumption, Customs Value, Actual U.S. dollars

HTS Description	2007	2008	Jan. – May 2008	Jan – May 2009
27090020 – Petroleum oils, crude, testing 25 degrees A.P.I. or more	48,117,120, 550	63,444,494, 090	27,244,208, 997	10,183,251, 411
27090010 – Petroleum oils, crude, testing under25 degrees A.P.I.	2,762,071, 085	3,877,336, 897	1,592,600, 433	781,003, 768
87032300 - Motor cars and other motor vehicles for transport of persons	438,676,528	1,572,007,113	657,522,081	582,536,191
27101905 – Distillate and residual fuel oil (including blends)	1,186,106, 069	1,864,277, 592	773,352, 542	342,159, 600
18010000 – Cocoa beans, whole or broken, raw or roasted	409,282, 750	589,312, 128	375,425, 656	290,948, 344
71023900 – Nonindustrial diamonds, worked, but not mounted or set	779, 358,051	862, 430,835	331,473,838	255,816 ,093
71101100 – Platinum, unwrought or in powder form	1,721, 839,898	1,284346, 223	666, 834,629	179, 522,029
26121000 – Uranium ores and concentrates	147,540, 085	245,142, 014	58,548, 065	162, 603.125

Source: U.S. International Trade Commission Trade Dataweb, http://dataweb .usitc.gov.

Notes: Harmonized Tariff Schedule (HTS) descriptions have been abbreviated where necessary to conform to table constraints.

The act stated that the President was to direct certain top officials to host the first Forum meeting with their counterparts from AGOA-eligible countries and countries attempting to meet AGOA eligibility requirements [40]. The purpose of the Forum is to "discuss expanding trade and investment relations between the United States and Sub-Saharan Africa and the implementation of

[AGOA]. including encouraging joint ventures between small and large businesses."

AGOA also required the President to encourage non-governmental organizations and the private sector to hold similar annual meetings, and it required the President to instruct U.S. delegates to the Forum to promote a review of HIV/AIDS in each Sub-Saharan African country and the effect on economic development. It required the President to meet, to the extent practicable, with heads of governments of Sub-Saharan African countries at least every two years to discuss expanding trade and investment relations, and the first such meeting should be within one year of enactment.

AGOA was enacted May 18, 2000, and almost a year later, on May 16, 2001, President Bush established the Forum and announced plans for its first meeting in Washington in October 2001. The first Forum was held October 29-3 0, 2001, in Washington, DC. President Bush addressed the Forum and announced several initiatives: (1) a $200 million Overseas Private Investment Corporation (OPIC) support facility to give U.S. firms access to loans, guarantees, and political risk insurance for investment projects; (2) a regional office of the Trade and Development Agency (TDA) in Johannesburg to help attract new investment; and (3) the Trade for African Development and Enterprise Program, initially funded at $15 million, to establish regional hubs to help African businesses in the global market. (These initiatives were implemented; see later sections.)

The second Forum was held January 13-17, 2003, in Port Louis, Mauritius. In a videotaped message, President Bush announced that he would ask Congress to extend AGOA beyond its 2008 deadline. He also outlined other U.S. support for Africa, including assignment of U.S. agricultural officials to the regional business hubs established after the first Forum; a FY2004 budget request for a 50% increase in development assistance; and an additional $200 million over five years for education and teacher training to the region.

The third Forum was held December 9-10, 2003, in Washington, DC. The fourth Forum took place in Dakar, Senegal, from July 18-20, 2005. President Bush addressed the fourth Forum through videotaped remarks, and he announced the African Global Competitiveness Initiative, which was to provide $200 million over the next five years to improve the competitiveness of African countries and build their capacity to trade. The fifth Forum was held June 6-7, 2006, in Washington, DC. The sixth Forum was held in Accra, Ghana, July 18-19, 2007.

For the first time, the sixth Forum combined all three sectors (government, private, and civil society) into one meeting. The seventh AGOA Forum was held in Washington, DC, on July 14-16, 2008, and focused on creating a business climate that will encourage private investment and help mobilize capital to finance investment.

The eighth AGOA Forum, to be held in Nairobi, Kenya, is scheduled for August 4-6, 2009.

Table 4. Leading U.S. Imports from Sub-Saharan Africa Entering Under the AGOA Preference Imports for Consumption, Customs Value, actual U.S. dollars

HTS Description	2007	2008	Jan – May 2008	Jan.-May 2009
27090020 – Petroleum oils, crude, testing 25 degrees A.P.I. or more	37,116,787, 647	48,518,019, 968	21,258, 903,991	6,914,286, 748
27090010 – Petroleum oils, crude, testing under 25 degrees A.P.I	1,771,945, 820	2,731,811, 660	1,030,626, 728	556,518, 320
87032300 - Motor cars and other motor vehicles for transport of persons not over3000cc	438,489, 364	1,553,389, 022	638,931, 711	582,536, 191
27101905 – Distillate and residual fuel oil	665,351, 614	750,982, 539	299,138, 420	72,710, 776
27101125 – Napthas from petroleum oils and bituminous materials	492,842, 636	658,853, 842	279,721, 906	67,140, 715
72021150 – Ferromangananese containing by weight more than 4% of carbon	149,736, 133	367,406, 195	143,855 ,956	42,954, 182
62046240 – Women's or girls' trousers, breeches, and shorts, not knitted or crocheted, of cotton	254,489,796	256,791,659	84,983,387	80,309,074
87032400 Motorcars and other motor vehicles for transport of persons, over3000cc	192,956	256,791,659	63,780,594	17,556,675
61103030 – Sweaters and pullovers, knitted or crocheted	225,374,660	161,602,238	55,397,756	37,847,579

Source: U.S. International Trade Commission Trade Dataweb, http://dataweb.usitc.gov.

Notes: Harmonized Tariff Schedule (HTS) descriptions have been abbreviated where necessary to conform to table constraints.

TECHNICAL ASSISTANCE AND CAPACITY BUILDING

AGOA legislation also directed the President to target U.S. government technical assistance and trade capacity building in AGOA beneficiary countries (Sec. 122). This mandate includes assistance to both government and non-governmental actors. The act directs the President to target technical assistance to governments—(1) to liberalize trade and exports; (2) to harmonize laws and regulations with WTO membership; (3) to engage in financial and fiscal restructuring; and (4) to promote greater agribusiness linkages. The act also includes assistance for developing private sector business associations and networks among U.S. and Sub-Saharan African enterprises. Technical assistance is also to be targeted to increasing the number of reverse trade missions, increasing trade in services, addressing critical agricultural policy issues, and building capabilities of African states to participate in the World Trade Organization, generally, and particularly in services. In FY2007 (latest available data), the United States reported obligating approximately $505 million in trade capacity building (TCB) assistance to Sub-Saharan Africa, up from $401 million in 2006. Cumulative U.S. TCB from FY2001 to FY2007 amounted to almost $1.6 billion [41]. The Millennium Challenge Corporation (MCC) accounted for about $376 million (74 percent) of FY2007 TCB assistance for SSA [42].

U.S. Agency for International Development (USAID)

AGOA's mandate to encourage trade-related technical assistance is primarily implemented by USAID through the African Global Competitiveness Initiative (AGCI), a Presidential Initiative which supplanted the Trade for African Development and Enterprise (TRADE) initiative in 2006. The TRADE initiative had supplanted the Africa Trade and Investment Policy Program (ATRIP), which operated from 1998 to 2003. These initiatives are generally used to focus activities around a common goal, but there are AGOA-related activities that are funded by other initiatives within USAID.

USAID funds various technical assistance programs throughout Africa aimed at improving trade within the region and between the region and the United States. USAID supports regional efforts through its regional missions and the four Regional Hubs for Global Competitiveness (Trade Hubs), located in Ghana, Senegal, Kenya, and Botswana. USAID bilateral missions support projects in individual African countries. The missions and hubs work on improving trade policy both regionally and within country governments. They also have programs to improve trade infrastructure, such as in transportation and energy, and they have enterprise development programs which often target specific industries, such as handicrafts and shea butter.

As mentioned above, AGOA encourages the establishment of private sector linkages between U.S. and SSA businesses. To this end, USAID funds an international business linkage program, South African International Business Linkages (SAIBL), which is implemented by the Corporate Council on Africa. SAIBL assists black-owned South African companies to prepare business plans, achieve International Standards Organization (ISO) certification, participate in U.S.-led trade delegations, attend trade shows in the United States, and identify public and private sector export financing. It also assists U.S. firms by identifying trade and investment opportunities in South Africa, by steering U.S. firms to appropriate government and private sector contacts, and by identifying sources of financing. USAID used to fund a similar linkage program for West Africa, the West African International Business Linkages (WAIBL), but it no longer funds this program. The regional trade hubs implement many of the same types of activities as SAIBL, except that they focus more on promoting trade in general and not just exports to the United States.

Assistant U.S. Trade Representative for Africa (AUSTRA)

Sec. 117 of AGOA supported the creation of this position to serve as the "primary point of contact in the executive branch for those persons engaged in trade between the United States and Sub- Saharan Africa," and the chief adviser to the U.S. Trade Representative (USTR) on trade and investment issues pertaining to Africa. This position previously had been established by President Clinton in 1998. One primary function of AUSTRA is to make the yearly determinations as to which countries are eligible for AGOA benefits generally, and also its special textile and apparel benefits. The AUSTRA also sponsors projects for WTO training for SSA trade negotiators, provides support for the Trade Advisory Committee on Africa, and maintains the http://www.agoa.gov website. The AUSTRA produced the AGOA Competitiveness Report, which was submitted to Congress on July 13, 2005. Mandated by the AGOA Acceleration Act of 2004, this report provides an analysis of potential economic growth sectors in Africa, barriers to growth in those sectors, and recommendations for U.S. technical assistance to assist in overcoming those barriers [43].

Overseas Private Investment Corporation (OPIC)

Since the enactment of AGOA, Sub-Saharan Africa has been one of OPIC's stated priorities. At the end of 2005, 15% of OPIC's total portfolio was in the region. As of May 2008, OPIC's exposure in the region was more than $2 billion [44]. In FY2006, OPIC supported 14 projects in SSA, or 20% of the year's 70 projects in total. OPIC has focused on projects to strengthen the region's basic financial infrastructure and housing sectors [45].

OPIC works in Africa and globally through three basic products including political risk insurance, finance (loan guarantees and direct loans), and investment funds. In 2005, OPIC provided $250 million in financing to establish two private equity investment funds in Africa. The first of these new funds is managed by Emerging Markets Partnership (EMP), and it targets infrastructure investments and related industries in Africa. The second fund, Ethos Fund V, aims to promote the expansion of medium-sized enterprises in Sub-Saharan Africa, emphasizing South Africa and the manufacturing and services sectors. These funds are in addition to three funds currently supported by OPIC, which are the $20 million Africa Growth Fund, the $110 million Modern Africa Growth and Investment Fund, and the ZM Africa Investment Fund. As initially planned, all three of these latter funds are currently divesting their assets.

Export-Import Bank (Ex-Im)

AGOA expressed the sense of Congress that the Ex-Im Bank should continue to expand its financial commitments to its loan guarantee and insurance programs to African countries. The legislation also commended the Bank's Sub-Saharan Africa Advisory Committee for its work in fostering economic cooperation between the United States and SSA. This committee was reauthorized to September 30, 2011 (P.L. 109-438) [46]. The 2006 legislation reauthorizing the Bank reaffirmed the SSA mandate, and also required the Bank to report annually on its efforts to improve its working relationship with the African Development Bank and other African institutions [47].

The Ex-Im Bank does not finance imports into the United States. However, it does provide loans and guarantees for U.S. exports to the region, some of which can be used to manufacture goods eligible for import to the United States under AGOA. This financing can cover manufacturing equipment, the purchase of U.S. fabric, yarn, and thread necessary for eligibility under AGOA textile provisions, or other raw materials or components used for manufacturing. Ex-Im operates in all 48 SSA countries, although Bank activity and eligibility for specific programs vary according to risk factors. In FY2007, Ex-Im Bank authorized 127 transactions totaling about $424 million in 18 SSA countries. According to its estimates, Ex-Im Bank covered approximately 3.1% of the total $14.1 billion of U.S. exports to SSA. By contrast, Ex-Im typically covers about 1% of U.S. exports worldwide [48]. In FY2006, Africa accounted for about 2.8% of the total authorizations of the Bank. At the end of the fiscal year, Ex-Im Bank's exposure in SSA was about $2.5 billion, or 4.3% of its total global exposure [49]. By contrast in FY2002, Africa accounted for 2.3% of the loan guarantees and 5% of the medium-term insurance instruments supported by the Bank with a total exposure of $3.2 billion [50].

In order to increase its lending activities in Africa, the Bank began its Africa Pilot Program (STIPP) in 1999 to provide short-term export credit to Sub-Saharan African countries, many of whom are not eligible for other Ex-Im financial instruments. This program was initially funded at $100 million. Ex-Im also announced in 2000 a pilot program to provide export credits to African countries to purchase U.S. HIV/AIDS medicines [51]. This program allows countries to extend payment of these pharmaceutical purchases to five years from standard repayment terms of six months. These export credits have covered two contracts valued at $15 million for medicines and HIV detection equipment to Nigeria and Togo [52]. In addition, the Bank reported that as a result of Paris Club sovereign debt restructuring negotiations, it had entered into agreements to restructure or to forgive public sector debt obligations totaling $92 million with eight Sub-Saharan African nations in FY2002. These agreements wrote off all of the Bank's public sector debt exposure in Mozambique, Tanzania, and Uganda [53].

U.S. and Foreign Commercial Service (USFCS)

In Sec. 125 of AGOA, Congress found that USFCS presence in SSA had been reduced since the 1980s and that the level of staffing in 1997 (seven officers in four countries) did not "adequately service the needs of U.S. businesses attempting to do business in Sub-Saharan Africa" [54].

Accordingly, the legislation required the posting of at least 20 USFCS officers in not less than 10 countries in SSA by December 31, 2001 "subject to the availability of appropriations" [55]. USFCS was instructed by Congress to open offices in Ghana and Senegal, with the stipulation that additional funds would be added to its overall budget. According to a USFCS official, these additional funds never materialized. Presently, USFCS has nine officers in six SSA countries: Côte d'Ivoire, Ghana, Kenya, Nigeria, Senegal, and South Africa. Commercial Service officers seek to facilitate the development of markets for U.S. exporters in the countries where they are stationed. Officers assisting U.S. exporters provide evaluations of potential business partners in the country, facilitate U.S. business contacts with local firms, identify potential local distributors or agents of U.S. exports, provide local financing options, and arrange partner background checks. Commercial Service officers also prepare the Country Commercial Guides which chronicle the business environment of the country.

Sec. 125(c) of the legislation directs the International Trade Administration (ITA) to develop an initiative (a) to identify the best U.S. export prospects to the region; (b) to identify tariff and non- tariff barriers that impede U.S. exports to Africa; and (c) undertake discussions with African states to increase market access for these goods and services. This activity is being carried out by the ITA in its Market Access and Compliance Unit (MAC). The Unit states that U.S. firms face entrenched tariff and other trade barriers in many African countries, and that its current staff of nine staffers is not adequate to cover the SSA region. In FY2003, MAC was given budget authority to add four analysts and negotiators to address these issues [56].

Trade and Development Agency (TDA)

Although not tasked with specific directives in AGOA, the TDA contributes to trade capacity building in Africa by funding project planning studies, including feasibility studies, training programs and orientation visits (reverse trade missions in which foreign government officials visit U.S. manufacturers). TDA targets activities that could generate significant U.S. export potential, that could facilitate access to natural resources important to the United States, and that are a priority for host nations and international development efforts. In FY2006, TDA obligated funds for 62 projects in SSA for a total of $10.6 million, or approximately 22% of its program expenditures [57].

Multilateral Initiatives

In addition to domestic agency programs, the United States participates in several multilateral institutions that provide trade capacity building in Africa and other developing-country regions. The World Bank and regional development banks all provide trade capacity building assistance, mainly in the form of loans.

The Integrated Framework (IF) is the main multilateral initiative in trade capacity building. It is a process that assists Least Developed Countries (LDCs) to integrate trade issues into their national development strategies. The IF process begins with a diagnostic study of trade challenges and opportunities in the LDC, and is meant to result in better targeted and coordinated assistance by all donors.

Six international institutions collaborate on the IF, including the International Monetary Fund (IMF), the International Trade Center (ITC), the United Nations Conference on Trade and Development (UNCTAD), the United Nations Development Program (UNDP), the World Bank, and the WTO. The IF is funded by an IF Trust Fund, composed of voluntary contributions from multilateral and bilateral donors. Total contributions to this trust fund equaled $49.66 million as of March 2007, of which the United States contributed $800,000 [58].

As of November 2007, 23 of the 29 LDCs that had completed the IF trade diagnostic process were in Sub-Saharan Africa. An additional six SSA countries (out of 11 total) had started the diagnostic process, and three more (out of five total) were under consideration to begin the IF process.

Several issues have been raised with regard to the IF. The IF was established partly to achieve greater donor coordination, and it is not yet clear whether it will have this effect.

In many countries, coordination is an ad hoc activity, achieved as a result of personal relationships rather than through institutional coordination. Thus far, IF work has centered on preparing strategies for trade capacity building, and there has been little coordinated implementation of these strategies [59]. Another concern is that the IF process has raised expectations among the participating LDCs, and these expectations may not be fulfilled by the IF process.

The United States has also provided SSA countries with technical assistance and TCB support on a wide range of WTO-related issues such as trade facilitation, services, and sanitary and phytosanitary measures in coordination with the other multilateral institutions mentioned above [60].

The United States has also provided technical support for the efforts of some SSA countries, such as Ethiopia (still in negotiations) and Tonga (WTO accession July 2007) to accede to the WTO [61].

Regional Cooperation and Free Trade Agreements

AGOA declares the policy position that free trade agreements (FTAs) should be negotiated, where feasible, between interested countries in SSA and the United States in order to serve as a catalyst for increasing trade and investment. Regional economic agreements among SSA countries are also encouraged in AGOA.

Discussion of potential partners for free-trade agreements has revolved around South Africa and SACU, but several other regional groupings may prove to be partners for future trade agreements with the United States. The Southern African Development Community (SADC), the Common Market for Eastern and Southern Africa (COMESA), the East African Community (EAC), and the West African Economic and Monetary Union (UEMOA) have all taken steps to begin the process of economic integration, either through trade liberalization or through steps to promote monetary union. While these groups are being encouraged in their attempts at regional integration, they are not immediate prospects for FTAs with the United States. Background on these groups appears in an Appendix.

FTA Negotiations with the Southern African Customs Union FTA (SACU) [62]

On November 4, 2002, then-USTR Robert B. Zoellick notified Congress that negotiations would be initiated with the members of the Southern African Customs Union (SACU). These negotiations began in June 2003, and were postponed indefinitely in April 2006. The United States and SACU reportedly could not agree on the scope and level of ambition of the negotiations. In addition, given SSA's generally low levels of economic, administrative, and regulatory development, many countries in the region are not yet in the position to enact the types of policies and reforms that would be required for a comprehensive FTA with the United States [63]. However, an FTA reportedly remains the long-term objective of both the United States and the SACU [64].

Currently, the United States and SACU are continuing talks for a Trade, Investment, and Development Cooperation Agreement (TIDCA), which may lead to an eventual FTA. The scope of the TIDCA is undefined, and may focus on some of the "behind the border" issues from the FTA negotiations, such as intellectual property rights and investment issues. The United States does not have a TIDCA with any other country or group. A TIDCA may proceed without extension of Trade Promotion Authority (TPA) [65], because it does not include the market access provisions of an FTA.

SACU is a customs union composed of South Africa, Botswana, Lesotho, Namibia, and Swaziland. The original SACU agreement dates from the colonial government in 1910 and was renegotiated with the apartheid government in 1969. A new agreement to more fully integrate the smaller states into decision-making for the area, which was previously dominated by South Africa, was signed on October 21, 2002. The agreement is characterized by free movement of goods within SACU, a common external tariff, and the common revenue pool which is apportioned among the member states.

A large degree of economic integration exists among the SACU states because of the agreement, perhaps contributing to the U.S. decision to negotiate an FTA with SACU, rather than just South Africa. However, South Africa is the dominant economy of the region, accounting for 87% of the population, and 92% of the gross domestic product of the customs area. U.S. merchandise exports to SACU totaled $4.6 billion in 2006, led by aircraft, vehicles, construction and agricultural equipment, and computers. U.S. merchandise imports from SACU totaled $8.4 billion, and were composed of minerals such as platinum, diamonds, titanium, iron and steel, textiles and apparel, vehicles, and automotive parts [66].

U.S. Trade and Investment Framework Agreements (TIFA)

The USTR regards TIFAs as important tools for strengthening economic relations with key SSA countries and regional organizations [67].

As of September 2007, the United States has negotiated TIFAs with Ghana, Liberia, Mauritius, Mozambique, Nigeria, Rwanda, and South Africa, and with the COMESA and UEMOA regional arrangements. Generally, TIFAs commit the signatories to expand trade of goods and services, to encourage private sector investment, and to resolve problems and disputes through consultation and dialogue. To facilitate these objectives, the signatories of each agreement have established a Council on Trade and Investment to provide a venue for consultation on trade issues of interest or concern to the parties, and to work toward the removal of impediments to trade and investment flows. TIFAs are often considered to be first steps to the negotiation of free trade agreements.

U.S. Bilateral Investment Treaties (BIT)

BITs help protect U.S. foreign direct investment and promote economic growth by advancing important reforms and encouraging the adoption of liberal policies that facilitate and support foreign investment [68]. As of September 2007, the United States has signed BITs with Cameroon, Republic of the Congo (Brazzaville), Democratic Republic of the Congo (Kinshasa), Mozambique, and Senegal. The goals of the BIT are to protect U.S. investments abroad, and to encourage market-oriented domestic policy in host countries. Generally, BITs ensure national treatment for U.S. investments, limits on expropriations, free repatriation of funds, limitations on the imposition of trade-distorting or inefficient practices on U.S. investments—including requirements in hiring—and the right of submission of investment disputes to international arbitration. These treaties are promoted by the U.S. government as a method of encouraging the development of international law and trade standards within the partner country.

New Partnership for Africa's Development (NEPAD)

NEPAD is a key policy vehicle of the African Union (AU), whose leaders formulated and adopted the initiative in July 2001. Described by its proponents as a multi-sector, sustainable development policy framework, NEPAD seeks to reduce poverty, increase economic growth, and improve socio-economic development prospects across Africa. Major NEPAD aims are to attract greater investment and development aid to Africa, reduce the continent's debt levels, and broaden global market access for African exports. NEPAD emphasizes increased democratization, political accountability, and transparency in governance in African states as primary means of achieving its goals [69].

European Union Activity

By way of comparison, the European Union (EU) has also been active in promoting trade between itself and the countries of Sub-Saharan Africa. The EU-South Africa Agreement on Trade, Development, and Cooperation entered into force on January 1, 2000. This agreement creates a free-trade area between the participants during a 12-year asymmetric transition period. The EU pledges to remove tariffs on 95% of imports from South Africa during a 10-year period with most products granted duty-free status in 2002. South Africa will remove duties on 86% of its tariff lines during a 12-year period with most eliminations occurring between 2006-20 12. Notably, the agreement does not provide tariff relief to several important South African agricultural exports, nor to aluminum.

The Cotonou Agreement, signed in Cotonou, Benin between the European Union and 71 African, Caribbean, and Pacific nations (ACP) in February 2000, extends non-reciprocal, duty-free access for industrial and processed agricultural goods to the EU market granted by the 4th Lomé Convention to the end of 2007. The extent of the duty-free access conferred by Cotonou was subsequently enhanced in March 2001 by the "Everything but Arms" initiative, which granted LDCs tariff-free access to all goods, except for sugar, rice, and bananas, for which products a tariff-rate quota system will be maintained during a phase-out period ending in 2009. Provisions of the Cotonou Agreement call for the negotiation of trade liberalization agreements with regional economic partnerships that could include the regional African groupings discussed in the Appendix. Preliminary negotiations on the Regional Economic Partnership Agreements (EPAs) began on September 27, 2002 and were supposed to conclude before the expiration of the Cotonou Agreement on December 31, 2007. Many African countries opposed signing EPAs because that would mean opening up their markets to EU imports. In the end, a temporary compromise was reached: most African countries signed "interim EPAs" to keep their EU trade preferences as they were under the Cotonou Agreement.

AGOA: Current and Future Challenges

Several issues may be important to Congress in the oversight of AGOA. These issues concern the termination of the WTO Multi Fiber Agreement, the diversification of beneficiary country and industry participants, the continued eligibility of certain countries for AGOA benefits, the HIV/AIDS epidemic, and the participation of U.S. small business in AGOA.

- *Termination of the Multi Fiber Agreement.* Article 2 of the WTO's Agreement on Textiles and Clothing (ATC) terminated the worldwide system of quotas for textile and apparel trade on January 1, 2005. Observers expressed concern that this would spell the end of the African apparel assembly industry, because African producers would be unable to compete on world markets without the quota-free advantage. After the ATC termination, apparel exports under AGOA declined, but the industry has not been completely decimated. One explanation for this is that the United States still imposes tariffs averaging 18% on most apparel articles, which gives AGOA beneficiaries an advantage [70].
- *Diversification of AGOA Exports.* While textile and manufacturing industries make up a growing part of U.S. imports under AGOA, these imports are dwarfed by AGOA imports from the petroleum and mining sectors. These industries are highly capitalized and do not provide extensive employment opportunities for African workers. AGOA benefits are also concentrated in few countries. Moreover, several AGOA-eligible countries export very little under the program. If a goal of the program is to increase African country participation, it may be achieved through continued targeted trade capacity building and technical assistance. Agriculture is an important source of income for African workers, and increasing agriculture exports under AGOA could help raise incomes and spur economic growth. African countries may also begin to export light manufactures, with improved capacity, infrastructure, and policies to encourage investment.
- *Eligibility Standards.* A country's eligibility for AGOA benefits may become a subject of controversy. Some observers feel that the President must strictly enforce eligibility requirements to ensure continued adherence to reforms. However, others have cited the unpredictability of a country's AGOA benefits from year to year as a

source of investment risk, and have suggested minimum eligibility terms of greater than the current one year. Another suggestion includes allowing Congress to override the President's decision to terminate AGOA benefits through legislation. Several countries have been considered candidates for losing AGOA eligibility. In December 2003, the President declared Eritrea and the Central African Republic to be ineligible for AGOA. In December 2004, Cote d'Ivoire was declared ineligible as well. Lesotho, which is considered an AGOA success story, has been the subject of persistent complaints from indigeous labor groups regarding working conditions in newly developed textile plants. Swaziland has received warnings from the State Department that its human rights record does not meet AGOA eligibility requirements. As of January 1, 2009, Mauritania was removed from AGOA eligibility. Several countries have questionable commitment to privatization and tariff reform.

- *HIV/AIDS.* The HIV/AIDS pandemic continues to destabilize the economies of Africa and threatens any progress achieved by AGOA as additional income is spent, not to raising living standards, but to treat a population afflicted with the disease. Due to the disease, life expectancy is falling in several AGOA-eligible countries and in the region as a whole. Even with the advantages that AGOA preferences confer, investors may be deterred from the region by high medical costs, by constant replacement of workers stricken with the disease and the attendant training costs, and by the destabilizing risks associated with a society containing a large, dying population.
- *Small Business Participation.* Small business accounts for about 55% of the U.S. GDP, and employs a large portion of American workers. U.S. small businesses, however, only participate in limited trade with Africa, and reportedly very few in the small business community know about AGOA. Some observers have noted that U.S. small businesses may benefit from AGOA, and in the process help provide avenues for diversifying African exports. Small business is also important in Africa, and increased partnership may result in better participation on both continents. The U.S. government could become involved in increasing awareness of AGOA among the small business community, and providing opportunities for partnership.

APPENDIX. REGIONAL ECONOMIC INTEGRATION AMONG SUB-SAHARA AFRICA NATIONS

Southern African Development Community (SADC)

This group is composed of the nations of Angola, Botswana, Democratic Republic of the Congo, Lesotho, Madagascar, Malawi, Mauritius, Mozambique, Namibia, South Africa, Swaziland, Tanzania, Zambia, and Zimbabwe. Originally formed by front-line states to lessen economic dependence on the apartheid regime in South Africa, the group expanded to include South Africa in 1994. The 1996 Protocol on Trade committed each signatory to remove duties and non-tariff barriers to SADC members within 12 years, to provide national treatment for each other's goods, and to bind existing tariffs at current levels.

The economic dominance of South Africa makes economic integration of the SADC region more problematic. South Africa accounts for 82% of the GDP of the region, and it comprises 62% of the region's intra-SADC imports and 70% of the SADC region's exports [71]. With per-capita income at approximately $3,000, it dwarfs the average per-capita income of many of the other states. In addition, smaller states within SADC are concerned about their lack of economic competitiveness as their home markets are opened up to goods from South Africa. The reliance of many governments on duty revenue has also become a source of concern in implementing reductions of tariff barriers.

Common Market for Eastern and Southern Africa (COMESA)

Founded in 1982 as the Preferential Trade Area of Eastern and Southern Africa, current member states of the COMESA include Angola, Burundi, Comoros, Democratic Republic of the Congo, Djibouti, Egypt, Eritrea, Ethiopia, Kenya, Libya, Madagascar, Malawi, Mauritius, Rwanda, Seychelles, Sudan, Swaziland, Uganda, Zambia and Zimbabwe. On October 31, 2000, nine states of COMESA (Djibouti, Egypt, Kenya, Madagascar, Malawi, Mauritius, Sudan, Zambia and Zimbabwe) launched a free trade area that eliminated tariffs on goods originating in the member states. These states have also worked towards establishing coordinated policies in other areas such as rules-of-origin, dispute settlement, applications of safeguard measures, and uniform customs procedures. The group agreed on a common external tariff in May 2007, and as of May 2008, 13 COMESA countries had joined the COMESA Free Trade Area and eliminated tariffs on all items produced in member countries [72]. The goal of monetary union by 2025 is expected to be advanced by the introduction of limited currency convertibility and improved coordination of fiscal and monetary policy during this time period.

East African Community (EAC)

Comprised of Kenya, Uganda, and Tanzania, this organization seeks to revive historic tariff-free trade that had been established among the three British colonies in 1923. However, this cooperation broke down in the 1970s due to widespread transshipments and the varied economic paths of its participants. The three countries re-established the community in 1999 and have made plans for an asymmetric tariff schedule, in which Kenya will immediately reduce its tariff to zero, while Uganda and Tanzania will have four years in which to reciprocate. The outlook for this grouping is also complicated by a dominant country presence. Most industrial trade in the bloc originates from Kenya, and there is little bilateral trade between Tanzania and Uganda. Nonetheless, two neighboring countries, Rwanda and Burundi, have been invited to join.

West African Economic and Monetary Union (UEMOA)

This grouping was originally created to administer the CFA franc (*Communauté financière africaine*), a currency formerly tied to the French franc prior to its disappearance in 2000 (it is still backed by the French treasury). Its members are Benin, Burkina Faso, Côte d'Ivoire, Mali, Niger, Senegal, Togo, and Guinea-Bissau, the sole non-francophone member. The member states have espoused the long-term goal of a full economic union with a common market, macroeconomic convergence, regulatory harmonization, and a common investment policy. A preferential tariff arrangement was concluded for member states in 1995, and a customs union with a common external tariff of 22% became operational in 2000. UEMOA countries have established a common accounting system, periodic reviews of member countries' macroeconomic policies, a regional stock exchange, and the legal and regulatory framework for a regional banking system [73]. Efforts are also being made to harmonize UEMOA with another regional bloc, the Economic Community of West African States (ECOWAS) [74].

ACKNOWLEDGMENT

This report was originally written by Danielle Langton.

REFERENCES

[1] Section 3108 of the Trade Act of 2002, P.L. 107-210.
[2] Section 6002 of the Tax Relief and Health Care Act of 2006, P.L. 109-432.
[3] A. Hoeffler, "The Augmented Solow Model and the African Growth Debate," CSAE, University of Oxford, March 2000.
[4] For a further discussion of African economic development, see CRS Report RL32489, *Africa: Development Issues and Policy Options*, by Raymond W. Copson.
[5] Jorge Saba Arbache and John Page, "Patterns of Long Term Growth in Sub-Saharan Africa." World Bank, November 2007.
[6] Jorge Saba Arbache and John Page, "More Growth or Fewer Collapses? A New Look at Long Run Growth in SSA." World Bank, October 2007.
[7] *The Economist*, May 13-19, 2000.
[8] L. Pritchett, "Patterns of Economic Growth: Hills, Plateaus, Mountains, and Plains," World Bank Paper, July 1998 (hereafter, Pritchett); http://www.worldbank.org/wbi/attackingpoverty/events/Turkey_0199/pritch.pdf.
[9] *Pritchett*, p. 18.
[10] W. Easterly, "Why Is Africa Marginal in the World Economy?," In G. Maasdrop, ed., *Can South and Southern Africa Become Globally Competitive Economies?* (New York: St Martin's Press, 1996), pp. 19-30.
[11] D. Rodrik, "Where Did All the Growth Go? External Shocks, Social Conflict and Growth Collapses," mimeo, London School of Economic and Political Science, August 1998.
[12] *Pritchett*, p. 12.
[13] The World Bank, *Africa Development Indicators 2007*, October 2007.

[14] The World Bank, *Global Development Finance,* 2006 and 2007.
[15] IHS Global Insight, World Overview Tables, Detailed Forecast Data, Second Quarter 2009.
[16] Economist Intelligence Unit. EIU Market Indicators and Forecasts Database. Inward direct investment are the net flows of direct investment capital by non-residents into the region.
[17] Ibid.
[18] Trade statistics are based on CRS calculations using the Global Trade Atlas Navigator database and the U.S. International Trade Commission Trade Dataweb.
[19] See CRS Report RL33584, *AIDS in Africa*, by Nicolas Cook.
[20] Joint United Nations Program on HIV/AIDS. *AIDS Epidemic Update*, December 2007.
[21] See CRS Report RL33584, *AIDS in Africa*, by Nicolas Cook. Data from World Bank, *African Development Indicators 2007.*
[22] International Monetary Fund, *World Economic Outlook Database,* October 2007.
[23] Ibid., and World Bank, *World Development Indicators Online,* October 16, 2006.
[24] International Monetary Fund, *World Economic Outlook Database,* October 2007.
[25] United States Trade Representative, *2008 Comprehensive Report on U.S. Trade and Investment Policy Toward Sub- Saharan Africa and Implementation of the African Growth and Opportunity Act*, May 2008.
[26] Global Trade Atlas Database.
[27] U.S. Department of Commerce, Bureau of Economic Analysis, International Economic Accounts, http://www.bea.gov/international/ di1usdbal.htm.
[28] Ibid.
[29] U.S. Department of Commerce, Bureau of Economic Analysis, "U.S. Direct Investment Abroad: Capital Outflows Without Current Cost Adjustment, 2008," *International Economic Accounts*, http://www.bea. gov.
[30] Ibid.
[31] Alliance to End Hunger, et al. Letter to House Ways and Means and Senate Finance Chairs and Ranking Members, April 22, 2009.
[32] "Levin Says Committee to Tackle Preference Reform After August Recess," *Inside U.S. Trade*, July 21, 2009.

[33] "ROZ Bill Stalls in Senate, Finance Committee Action Likely to Slip to Fall," *Inside U.S. Trade*, July 17, 2009.
[34] See CRS Report RL33663, *Generalized System of Preferences: Background and Renewal Debate*, by Vivian C. Jones.
[35] On March 6, 2001, the Chairman and Ranking Member of the House Ways and Means Committee and 8 other Members from both parties wrote to the Secretary of the Treasury saying that the U.S. Customs Service interpretation of benefits for knit-to-shape articles was "wrong." See, Text: Ways and Means AGOA Letter to O'Neill, *Inside U.S. Trade*, March 9, 2001.
[36] For more information, see CRS Report RS2271 8, Trade Adjustment Assistance for Workers (TAA) and Reemployment Trade Adjustment Assistance (RTAA), by John J. Topoleski.
[37] United States Trade Representative. 2008 Comprehensive Report on U.S. Trade and Investment Policy Toward Sub- Saharan Africa and Implementation of the African Growth and Opportunity Act, May 2008. (Hereinafter 2008 USTR SSA Report).
[38] CRS calculations based on data from the U.S. International Trade Commission Trade Dataweb, http://dataweb.usitc.gov
[39] Representatives from appropriate Sub-Saharan African regional organizations and government officials from other appropriate countries in Sub-Saharan Africa also could be invited
[40] 2008 USTR SSA Report, p. 43 42 Ibid.
[41] See AGOA Competitiveness Report, http://www.ustr.gov/assets/Document_Library/Reports_Publications/2005/asset_upload_file604_7857.pdf.
[42] 2008 USTR SSA Report, p. 70.
[43] Report of the Overseas Private Investment Corporation on the Host Country Development and U.S. Economic Effects of OPIC-Assisted Projects, Fiscal Year 2006. Submitted pursuant to Section 240A of the Foreign Assistance Act of 1961, as amended, March 2007
[44] Export-Import Bank Reauthorization Act, 12 U.S.C. 635(b)(9)(B)(iii).
[45] CRS Report RL33440, *Export-Import Bank: Reauthorization*, by James K. Jackson.
[46] Ex-Im Bank Africa Update, January 2008.
[47] Ex-Im Bank, 2006 Annual Report.
[48] Ex-Im Bank, 2002 Annual Report.
[49] See "Short-Term Africa Pilot Program," http://www.exim.gov/africa-i/afr02fac.html.

[50] Conversation with Export-Import Bank Official, February 6, 2003.
[51] Ex-Im, *2002 Annual Report*, p. 39.
[52] AGOA, Sec. 125(a)(4).
[53] AGOA, Sec. 125(b).
[54] International Trade Administration, "Budget Estimates FY2003," Exhibit 13, p. 65; Conversation with ITA official, March 6, 2003.
[55] U.S. Trade and Development Agency, 2006 Annual Report.
[56] See the Integrated Framework website, http://www.integrated framework.org.
[57] Susan Prowse, "Mega-Coherence: The Integrated Framework," *Trade and Aid: Partners or Rivals in Development Policy.* Cameron May: 2006.
[58] 2008 USTR Report, p. 40.
[59] Ibid
[60] For more information, see CRS Report RS21387, *United States-Southern African Customs Union (SACU) Free Trade Agreement Negotiations: Background and Potential Issues*, by Danielle Langton.
[61] 2008 USTR Report, p. 41.
[62] Ibid, p. 41.
[63] For more information on TPA renewal, see CRS Report RL33743, *Trade Promotion Authority (TPA): Issues, Options, and Prospects for Renewal*, by J. F. Hornbeck and William H. Cooper.
[64] U.S. International Trade Commission data website, at http://data web.usitc.gov
[65] 2008 USTR SSA Report, p. 42.
[66] Ibid.
[67] This paragraph was prepared by Nicolas Cook, Analyst in African Affairs. For more information, see CRS Report RS21353, *New Partnership for Africa's Development (NEPAD)*, by Nicolas Cook, and CRS Report RS21332, *The African Union*, by Nicolas Cook.
[68] For more information on the ATC, see CRS Report RL34106, *U.S. Clothing and Textile Trade with China and the World: Trends Since the End of Quotas*, by Michael F. Martin.
[69] Beverly M. Carl, *Trade and the Developing World in the 21st Century* (Ardsley, NY: Transnational Publishers, 2001), p. 205.
[70] 2008 USTR SSA Report, p. 37.
[71] 2008 USTR SSA Report, p. 39.
[72] Ibid.

In: U.S. Political and Trade Relations with Africa ISBN 978-1-61209-956-9
Editor: Gregory D. Ferro © 2012 Nova Science Publishers, Inc.

Chapter 2

AFRICA COMMAND: U.S. STRATEGIC INTERESTS AND THE ROLE OF THE U.S. MILITARY IN AFRICA*

Lauren Ploch

ABSTRACT

On February 6, 2007, the Bush Administration announced the creation of a new unified combatant command, U.S. Africa Command or AFRICOM, to promote U.S. national security objectives in Africa and its surrounding waters. Prior to AFRICOM's establishment, U.S. military involvement on the continent was divided among three commands: U.S. European Command (EUCOM), U.S. Central Command (CENTCOM), and U.S. Pacific Command (PACOM). The new command's area of responsibility (AOR) includes all African countries except Egypt. AFRICOM was officially launched as a sub-unified command under EUCOM on October 1, 2007, and became a stand-alone command on October 1, 2008.

In recent years, analysts and U.S. policymakers have noted Africa's growing strategic importance to U.S. interests. Among those interests are the increasing importance of Africa's natural resources, particularly energy resources, and mounting concern over violent extremist activities and other potential threats posed by uncontrolled spaces, such as piracy

---

*This is an edited, reformatted and augmented version of CRS Report RL34003, dated July 28, 2009.

and illicit trafficking. In addition, there is ongoing concern for Africa's many humanitarian crises, armed conflicts, and more general challenges, such as the devastating effect of HIV/AIDS. In 2006, Congress authorized a feasibility study on the creation of a new command for Africa to consolidate current operations and activities on the continent under one commander. Congress has closely monitored the command since its establishment.

As envisioned by the Department of Defense (DOD), AFRICOM aims promote U.S. strategic objectives by working with African states and regional organizations to help strengthen regional stability and security through improved security capability and military professionalizetion. If directed by national command authorities, its military operations would aim to deter aggression and respond to crises.

DOD signaled its intention to locate AFRICOM's headquarters on the continent early in the planning process, but such a move is unlikely to take place for several years, if at all. U.S officials are consulting with strategic partners in the region to determine what type of presence on the continent would be most appropriate, and what location, or locations, might be most suitable. The new command will operate from Stuttgart, Germany for the foreseeable future. DOD has stressed that there are no plans to have a significant troop presence on the continent. The East African country of Djibouti, home to the Combined Joint Task Force–Horn of Africa (CJTF-HOA), provides the U.S. military's only enduring infrastructure in Africa.

The 1998 bombing of U.S. embassies in East Africa, and more recent attacks, have highlighted the threat of terrorism to U.S. interests on the continent. Political instability and civil wars have created vast ungoverned spaces, areas in which some experts allege that terrorist groups may train and operate. Instability also heightens human suffering and retards economic development, which may in turn threaten U.S. economic interests. Africa's exports of crude oil to the United States are now roughly equal to those of the Middle East, further emphasizing the continent's strategic importance. This report provides a broad overview of U.S. strategic interests in Africa and the role of U.S. military efforts on the continent as they pertain to the creation of AFRICOM. A discussion of AFRICOM's mission, its coordination with other government agencies, and its basing and manpower requirements is included.

ISSUES FOR CONGRESS

President George W. Bush formally announced the creation of a new Unified Combatant Command (COCOM) for the African continent on February 6, 2007, reflecting Africa's increasing strategic importance to the

United States [1]. The Department of Defense (DOD) organizes its command structure by dividing its activities among joint military commands based either on a geographic or functional area of responsibility (AOR) [2]. With the creation of the new command, DOD now has six geographic commands and four functional commands. Previously, U.S. military involvement in Africa was divided among three geographic commands: European Command (EUCOM), Central Command (CENTCOM), and Pacific Command (PACOM). The new command's area of responsibility (AOR) includes all African countries except Egypt, which remains in the AOR of CENTCOM. Africa Command (AFRICOM) was launched with initial operating capability (IOC) as a sub-unified command under EUCOM on October 1, 2007 and reached full operating capability (FOC) as a stand-alone unified command on October 1, 2008. AFRICOM's first commander, Army General William E. "Kip" Ward, former Deputy Commander of EUCOM, was confirmed by the Senate on September 28, 2007.

Although the precise wording of AFRICOM's mission statement has evolved since the command was first announced, DOD officials have broadly suggested that the command's mission is to promote U.S. strategic objectives by working with African partners to help strengthen stability and security in the region through improved security capability and military professionalizetion [3]. A key aspect of the command's mission is its supporting role to other agencies' and departments' efforts on the continent. But like other combatant commands, AFRICOM will also be expected to oversee military operations, when directed, to deter aggression and respond to crises.

The Bush Administration's motivation for the creation of a new unified command for Africa evolved in part out of concerns about DOD's division of responsibility for Africa among three geographic commands, which reportedly posed coordination challenges. Although some military officials have advocated the creation of an Africa Command for over a decade, recent crises highlighted the challenges created by "seams" between the COCOMs' boundaries.

One such seam was located between Sudan (then within CENTCOM's AOR), Chad and the Central African Republic (then within EUCOM's AOR), an area of increased instability. The United States, acting first alone and later as a member of the North Atlantic Treaty Organization (NATO), has provided airlift and training for African peacekeeping troops in the Darfur region of Sudan, and although CENTCOM had responsibility for Sudan, much of the airlift and training was done by EUCOM forces.

In addition, close observers say that EUCOM and CENTCOM had become overstretched particularly given the demands created by the wars in Iraq and Afghanistan. The Commander of EUCOM, whose AOR included 92 countries prior to AFRICOM's creation, testified before Congress that

> the increasing strategic significance of Africa will continue to pose the greatest security stability challenge in the EUCOM AOR. The large ungoverned area in Africa, HIV/AIDS epidemic, corruption, weak governance, and poverty that exist throughout the continent are challenges that are key factors in the security stability issues that affect every country in Africa [4].

His predecessor, General James Jones, pointed out in 2006 that EUCOM's staff were spending more than half their time on Africa issues, up from almost none three years prior [5].

AFRICOM has faced myriad challenges in its establishment, and outstanding issues remain as the command moves forward. Some of these issues have been or may be addressed by the 111th Congress. Key oversight questions relating to the command may include the following.

- Is an Africa Command necessary or desirable? Is its mission well-defined?
- How are U.S. strategic interests influencing the size and scope of the U.S. military footprint on the continent, and what effect will the new command have on future U.S. military operations in Africa?
- How are AFRICOM and U.S. military efforts in Africa perceived by Africans and by other foreign countries, including China?
- What are the costs associated with AFRICOM? How are these costs affected by AFRICOM's chosen headquarters location?
- What role, if any, will contractors play in AFRICOM's operations?
- How closely do the State Department and DOD coordinate on plans for the command and on U.S. military efforts in Africa in general? What are the Obama Administration's views on the development of AFRICOM's interagency process? Does AFRICOM's enhanced integration of non-DOD USG agency personnel into the command necessitate statutory changes?
- How is AFRICOM addressing the intelligence community's need to realign its resources directed toward the continent?

- How will the Obama Administration ensure that U.S. military efforts in Africa do not overshadow or contradict U.S. diplomatic and development objectives? Should conflict prevention activities be an essential part of DOD's mandate, and are they sustainable?
- What are the authorities granted to U.S. Chiefs of Mission regarding combatant command activities in the countries to which they are posted, and are these authorities sufficient?
- How prominent will counter-terrorism operations and programs be, particularly relative to the peacekeeping training and support components in AFRICOM's mandate? Would some DOD-implemented counter-terrorism programs be more appropriately implemented by other U.S. agencies?
- Are the legal authorities guiding DOD's implementation of security cooperation reform programs sufficient? Do any of these authorities hinder the U.S. military's ability to conduct these programs?
- What efforts does DOD take to ensure that the training and equipment provided to African security forces are not used to suppress internal dissent or to threaten other nations?

This report provides information on AFRICOM's mission, structure, interagency coordination, and its basing and manpower requirements. The report also gives a broad overview of U.S. strategic interests in Africa and the role of U.S. military efforts on the continent as they pertain to the creation of Africa Command.

The DOD Proposal for a New Africa Command

Changes to the Unified Command Plan

The mission of geographic commands is defined by a general geographic area of responsibility (AOR), while the mission of functional commands is the worldwide performance of transregional responsibilities. There are currently six geographic combatant commands: Africa (AFRICOM), European (EUCOM), Pacific (PACOM), North (NORTHCOM), Southern (SOUTHCOM), and Central (CENTCOM) Commands. There are four functional COCOMs, including Transportation (TRANSCOM), Special Operations (SOCOM), Joint Forces (JFCOM) and Strategic (STRATCOM)

Commands. As mentioned above, DOD responsibilities for Africa were divided among three geographic commands prior to October 2008. EUCOM, based in Germany, had 42 African countries in its AOR; [6] CENTCOM, based in Florida, covered eight countries in East Africa, including those that make up the Horn of Africa; and PACOM, based in Hawaii, was responsible for the islands of Comoros, Madagascar, and Mauritius [7].

The creation of a new combatant command requires changes by the President to a classified executive document, the Unified Command Plan (UCP), which establishes responsibilities and areas of responsibilities for the commanders of combatant commands. Changes to the UCP are usually initiated by the Chairman of the Joint Chiefs of Staff (CJCS), who presents a recommendation to the Secretary of Defense.

After the Secretary's review, a proposal is presented to the President for approval. Prior to the advent of AFRICOM, the most recent Unified Command to be established was NORTHCOM, which was created in 2002, after the September 11 terrorist attacks, to protect the U.S. homeland. The UCP is reviewed at least every two years, as required by the Goldwater-Nichols DOD Reorganization Act of 1986 (P.L. 99-433). The 2006 review recommended the establishment of an Africa Command, and the 2008 review, released in December 2008, codified the command. A new functional command, Medical Command, is reportedly also being considered. Congress has, on occasion, taken legislative action that has led to changes in the UCP.

Combatant Command "Plus"?

Some DOD officials have referred to Africa Command as a combatant command "plus" [8]. This implies that the command has all the roles and responsibilities of a traditional geographic combatant command, including the ability to facilitate or lead military operations, but also includes a broader "soft power" mandate aimed at building a stable security environment and incorporates a larger civilian component from other U.S. government agencies to address those challenges. According to the 2002 U.S. National Security Strategy, "America is now threatened less by conquering states than we are by failing ones." The Department of Defense, identifying instability in foreign countries as a threat to U.S. interests, issued DOD Directive 3000.05 in 2005, defining stability operations [9] as a "core U.S. military mission" that "shall be given priority comparable to combat operations." [10]. The 2008 National Defense Strategy further argues that "the inability of many states to police themselves effectively or to work with their neighbors to ensure regional security represents a challenge to the international system" and that "if left unchecked, such instability can spread and threaten regions of interest to the United States, our allies, and friends." Although U.S. forces have traditionally focused on "fighting and winning wars," defense strategy is now evolving to look at conflict prevention, or "Phase Zero," addressing threats at their inception through increased emphasis on theater security cooperation (TSC) and capacity building of allies [11]. The Obama Administration's FY20 10 Budget Request reflects "a continued emphasis on leveraging 'soft power' and building the capacity of our partner nations." [12].

As General Bantz Craddock, former Commander of EUCOM, noted in his 2006 confirmation hearing, Africa in recent years had posed "the greatest security stability challenge" to EUCOM, and "a separate command for Africa would provide better focus and increased synergy in support of U.S. policy and engagement" [13]. In the view of AFRICOM's architects and proponents, if U.S. agencies, both military and civilian, are able to coordinate more efficiently and effectively both among themselves as well as with their African partners and other international actors, they might be more successful at averting more complex emergencies on the continent. The 2008 National Defense Strategy stresses the military's commitment to the concept of a new "Jointness," with emphasis on developing a "whole-of-government" approach toward meeting national security objectives, including greater civilian participation in military operations and greater harmonization of best practices among interagency partners. AFRICOM's commander, General Kip Ward, views the Department of Defense's role in Africa as part of a "three-pronged" U.S. government approach, with DOD, through AFRICOM, taking the lead on security issues, but playing a supporting role to the Department of State, which conducts diplomacy, and USAID, which implements development programs.

Ward does see AFRICOM playing a greater role in development activities than other commands, but has emphasized that its role will remain one of supporting USAID 's development and humanitarian objectives. Command guidance for AFRICOM's humanitarian and civic assistance activities stresses that such activities should compliment, not duplicate, other U.S. government activities, and should be used to strengthen security sector relationships. AFRICOM policies also require such activities to meet both US foreign policy objectives and AFRICOM theater strategic interests, and they must be approved by the Ambassador and USAID Mission Directorin the host country [14].

AFRICOM's proactive approach to deterring or averting conflict reflects an evolution in DOD strategy that has been outlined extensively in government documents, but operationalizing that broad mandate may prove difficult [15]. As one foreign policy expert points out, "the mission of AFRICOM will necessarily require a major break with conventional doctrinal mentalities both within the armed services themselves and between government agencies." [16]. One former DOD official described the mandate in the following words, "We want to help develop a stable environment in which civil society can be built and that the quality of life for the citizenry can be improved"[17]. The prospect that the Department of Defense will focus less on fighting wars and more on preventing them engenders mixed feelings elsewhere in the government. While many at the State Department and the United States Agency for International Development (USAID) welcome the ability of DOD to leverage resources and to organize complex operations, there also is concern that the military may overestimate its capabilities as well as its diplomatic role, or pursue activities that are not a core part of its mandate. Some argue that the highly unequal allocation of resources between the Departments of Defense, State, and USAID, hinder their ability to act as "equal partners" and could lead to the militarization of development and diplomacy [18].

The mission of Africa Command might be most closely compared to that of Southern Command (SOUTHCOM), which is responsible for U.S. military efforts in Central and South America. SOUTHCOM's mission, as defined by DOD, is to ensure the forward defense of the United States through security cooperation, counter-narcotics operations, humanitarian assistance, and monitoring and support for human rights initiatives in the region. Like SOUTHCOM, AFRICOM is expected to supervise an array of operations that relate to U.S. strategic interests but are not combat-related, unlike EUCOM, CENTCOM and PACOM, which have traditionally been more focused on preparing for potential warfighting operations. One DOD official suggested that the U.S. government could consider the command a success "if it keeps American troops out of Africa for the next 50 years" [19].

Interagency Coordination

The Bush Administration suggested that its proposal for AFRICOM represented an evolution in the involvement of other U.S. government agencies in the DOD planning process. Interagency coordination of U.S.

security policy involves a variety of offices and actors in Washington, DC, and in the field. In Washington, the State Department's Bureau of Political-Military Affairs (PM) serves as the primary liaison for the Department with DOD. Its counterpart at DOD is the Office of the Assistant Secretary of Defense for International Security Affairs (ISA). USAID created the Office of Military Affairs (OMA) within the Bureau for Democracy, Conflict and Humanitarian Assistance (DCHA) in 2005 to coordinate agency policy with DOD and the State Department for humanitarian relief and post conflict reconstruction efforts. USAID's Office of U.S. Foreign Disaster Assistance (OFDA), Operations Liaison Unit (OLU), and the geographic bureaus' missions manage the operational coordination with DOD for those activities.

At the regional level, State's PM Bureau appoints senior officials known as Foreign Policy Advisors (POLADs) to serve as advisors to combatant commanders and other military leaders to "provide policy support regarding the diplomatic and political aspects of the commanders' military responsibilities." [20]. Like the State Department, USAID places OFDA military liaison officers with COCOMs that routinely provide humanitarian and disaster relief coordination; OMA also currently has policy advisors known as Senior Development Advisors (SDAs) in several commands, including AFRICOM. The State Department, intelligence and other government agencies also designate representatives to Joint Interagency Coordination Groups (JIACGs) within the COCOMs to facilitate the interagency process. The JIACG is a relatively recent concept, created out of a request by former CENTCOM Commander General Tommy Franks in 2001 to "execute and influence policy, but not to make it, and to establish new interagency links, but not to replace habitual relationships or traditional chains of command." [21].

At the country level, DOD assigns senior defense officials/defense attachés (SDO/DATT) to serve as military liaisons at embassies around the world. These officials serve on interagency embassy Country Teams, which are led by the U.S. ambassador in each country. Many embassies also have an Office of Security Cooperation (OSC), which reports to the ambassador and the COCOM, to coordinate security assistance activities with the host country's defense forces [22]. USAID OFDA deploys military liaison officers as part of a Disaster Assistance Response Team (DART) to affected countries during humanitarian assistance and disaster relief operations when there is a civil-military component involved.

The new command has sought greater interagency coordination with the State Department, USAID, and other government agencies, including a larger non-DOD civilian staff (initially proposed at as much as one quarter of the total staff), than has been traditional with other combatant commands. Those involved in the creation of AFRICOM aimed to build upon initiatives in NORTHCOM and SOUTHCOM to improve the interagency process, but EUCOM Commander General Bantz Craddock has suggested that this command could be "the pioneer" for a new approach that the other commands might later adopt. In the development of AFRICOM's first theater strategy and supporting campaign plan, for example, the leadership sought to involve other U.S. government agencies at the earliest stages of the planning process, an effort that DOD hopes to employ more broadly as its new planning approach [23]. Non-DOD civilian staff positions within AFRICOM include senior leadership positions, senior advisors or liaisons (including the Foreign Policy Advisor, a Senior Development Advisor, an OFDA liaison, and a senior Treasury Department representative), and subject-matter experts embedded with the headquarters staff. During his confirmation hearing, General Ward testified that he did not believe any statutory changes were necessary to incorporate "detailed" non-DOD personnel into the command [24]. Officials report that filling those interagency positions has been more challenging than first anticipated. Although lawyers from several departments have worked to facilitate the assignment of non-DOD civilians to AFRICOM, less than 30 were permanently assigned in early 2009.

Following General Ward's confirmation, a senior U.S. diplomat, Ambassador Mary Carlin Yates, was appointed as Deputy to the Commander for Civil-Military Activities (DCMA), a new post equivalent to that of a deputy commander. Yates, who had previously served as U.S. ambassador to Burundi and Ghana and most recently as the Foreign Policy Advisor to EUCOM, was the first non-DOD civilian to be integrated into the command structure of a unified command. The DCMA directs many of AFRICOM's civil-military plans and programs, as well as its various security cooperation initiatives, and is responsible for ensuring that policy development and implementation are consistent with U.S. foreign policy. Ambassador Yates recently left AFRICOM to become the Senior Director for Strategic Planning and Institutional Reform at the National Security Council; the Department of State and AFRICOM are expected to announce her replacement soon.

Navy Vice Admiral Robert Moeller, who led AFRICOM's transition team, has served as Yates' military equivalent, Deputy to the Commander for Military Operations (DCMO). The DCMO is responsible for the implementation and execution of the command's programs and operations. To maintain the military chain of command, one deputy commander position will always be held by a military officer, but DOD statements suggest that AFRICOM's DCMA role will always be held by a Senior Foreign Service Officer [25].

Both Deputies have supervisory authority for the civilian and military personnel in their respective offices.

Structure and Footprint

DOD officials emphasize that the new command is still under development; some details regarding the command's structure and footprint are still being finalized. As mentioned above, AFRICOM's final headquarters location has not been identified, and a move to the continent may not occur for several years, if at all. DOD officials initially considered the establishment of sub- regional offices in Africa but reportedly received resistance from the State Department, based on concerns related to chief-of-mission authority. Officials stress that there are no plans to establish any new military bases in Africa; President Bush reiterated this during his visit to the continent in February 2008 [26]. Bush's Principal Under Secretary of Defense asserted that the creation of AFRICOM reflected an "organizational change," rather than a change in "basing structure or troop positions on the continent" [27].

At present, DOD's Combined Joint Task Force-Horn of Africa (CJTF-HOA) has a semipermanent troop presence at Camp Lemonier in Djibouti with more than 1,500 U.S. military and civilian personnel in residence. The U.S. military has a five year lease with the Djiboutian government for Lemonier, with the option to extend the lease for two more five-year terms. The command authority for CJTF-HOA, formerly under CENTCOM, has been transferred to AFRICOM, and it will continue to be used as an enduring Forward Operating Site [28]. AFRICOM's other Forward Operating Site is on the United Kingdom's Ascension Island in the south Atlantic. U.S. military facilities in Rota, Spain; Sionella, Italy; and Cairo, Egypt serve as logistic support facilities. The U.S. military also has access to a number of foreign air bases and ports in Africa and has established "bare-bones" facilities maintained by local troops in several locations. The U.S. military used facilities in Kenya in the 1990s to support its intervention in Somalia and continues to use them today to support counter-terrorism activities. DOD refers to these facilities as "lily pads," or Cooperative Security Locations (CSLs), and currently has access to locations in Algeria, Botswana, Gabon,

Ghana, Kenya, Mali, Namibia, Sao Tome and Principe, Sierra Leone, Tunisia, Uganda, and Zambia.

Headquarters Location

There has been considerable debate over where to ultimately base AFRICOM. Prior to AFRICOM's establishment, EUCOM was the only geographic combatant command with headquarters located outside of the United States. Given that the majority of countries in AFRICOM's AOR were previously under the responsibility of EUCOM, and that consequently a majority of the personnel working on Africa issues were already based in EUCOM's headquarters in Stuttgart, Germany, DOD determined that AFRICOM's headquarters would be initially located at the American base in Germany as well [29].

In November 2008, the Secretary of Defense announced that the decision on whether to move the command out of Germany would be postponed until 2012 to allow the command to gain greater understanding of its long-term operational requirements.

Prior to Secretary Gates' announcement of the command's establishment, there was speculation that an Africa Command might be permanently located in Europe, or in the United States, like the other commands. Some DOD officials have argued that AFRICOM's headquarters should be located in Africa. Locating the headquarters within the AOR would have several benefits in terms of proximity. Flight time from Germany to Nairobi, Kenya, for example, is approximately 8 hours, and flight time from Germany to Johannesburg, South Africa is approximately 11 hours. Flight time from Washington, DC to the African Union (AU) headquarters in Addis Ababa, Ethiopia is approximately 16-20 hours. Deploying AFRICOM's staff in close geographic proximity to their African counterparts and to U.S. diplomatic missions on the continent could enable more efficient interaction.

Those who have advocated locating Africa Command on the continent have faced some initial negative reactions from Africans. There are concerns, both domestically and internationally, that moving the command to Africa might be the first step in an alleged U.S. military agenda to establish a larger footprint on the continent. DOD officials stressed that the location in question would be a staff headquarters rather than a troop headquarters, and suggested that they might consider a dispersed regional headquarters model, with several small locations spread across the continent to lessen the U.S. presence and burden in any one country [30]. DOD may eventually try to co-locate those facilities with the headquarters of the continent's regional and sub-regional organizations to link AFRICOM with the AU's nascent regional security architecture (see "Security Assistance" below). AFRICOM already has military liaison officers (LNOs) at the African Union headquarters in Ethiopia and with ECOWAS in Nigeria, as well as at the Kofi Annan International Peacekeeping Training Center in Ghana.

Those presences are likely to expand, and additional liaison offices may be attached to other regional organizations. DOD's FY2009 budget request sought funding for a "limited presence on the African continent with the establishment of two of five regional offices," although plans for those two offices were postponed and funding for the offices was cut by Congress [31].

The Department of Defense has developed criteria for determining the ultimate location(s) for AFRICOM in coordination with the Department of State. Through regular consultations with African countries that have a security relationship with the United States, U.S. officials have reportedly received offers to host the command from several of these governments, including, most publicly, Liberia. Other strategic partners, such as South Africa and Algeria, have expressed reluctance to host the new command, possibly out of concern over a permanent foreign military presence within their borders. In North Africa, for example, there are concerns that an American military presence might embolden domestic terrorist groups. Some African governments that consider themselves to be regional hegemons may perceive a permanent American military presence, whether staffed by civilians or troops, to be a rival for political or military power in their sphere of influence.

At the forefront of DOD considerations in determining a host country (or countries) would be providing for the safety and security of over a thousand American personnel who staff the command and their families, should a decision to move to the continent be made. Living standards in Africa are among the lowest in the world, and DOD would be expected to choose a politically stable location on the continent with good access to health care and schools and relatively low levels of corruption.

Ease of access to regional and international transportation, along with proximity to the African Union, African regional organizations, and U.S. government hubs on the continent would also be considered. Locating U.S. soldiers permanently in a foreign country would be predicated on the host country's approval of a Status-of-Forces Agreement (SOFA), a legal document negotiated by the State Department to define the legal status of U.S. personnel and property while in that country, and a bilateral non-surrender agreement, commonly known as an Article 98 Agreement, to protect American servicemen from prosecution by the International Criminal Court [32].

Some advocacy groups hope that DOD would consider potential host countries' human rights record among other criteria. In testimony before the House Appropriations Defense Subcommittee in March 2009, however, AFRICOM's Commander, General Ward, indicated that while there was still a potential for the headquarters to be located in Africa, such a move was neither necessary nor sought after at this time [33].

Manpower

Manning a new command is a challenging task, particularly in a time when defense resources and personnel are stretched thin by engagements in Iraq and Afghanistan. While the number of personnel needed to staff a combatant command varies, DOD officials estimate that the average command ranges from 500 to more than 1,000 personnel (exclusive of supporting intelligence architecture) [34]. AFRICOM was authorized to have just over 1,300 headquarters staff by October 2008, including intelligence and other support requirements [35]. Sourcing manpower to facilitate the aggressive timeline to meet full operational capacity proved difficult, according to AFRICOM officials, and less than 75% of these positions were filled by the FOC date. Approximately 270 personnel for the new command were transferred from EUCOM, CENTCOM, and PACOM. The armed services (Army, Navy, Air Force, and Marines) are now in the process of standing up the service component headquarters that will support the new command; most expect to be fully operational by October 2009 [36]. In essence, the Services must pay two manpower bills—they must fill AFRICOM headquarters requirements and also staff the service component headquarters. Current service component headquarters proposals range from approximately 100 to 500 personnel [37]. U.S. Army Africa, for example, is expected to have 318 military and 110 civilian personnel at full operating capacity. The command's service components currently have no assigned forces and instead must rely on forces provided through the Global Force Management and Request for Forces system.

Cost

Start-up costs for Africa Command in FY2007 were approximately $51 million, and the nascent command's budget for Fiscal Year 2008 (October 1, 2007, to September 30, 2008) was estimated at $154.6 million. The Bush Administration's FY2009 budget request included $389 million for the command to cover 1) operation of the headquarters in Stuttgart, 2) an AFRICOM intelligence capability, 3) a Theater Special Operations Command (TSOC) for AFRICOM, 4) operational support aircraft, 5) the establishment of two regional offices on the continent (see above), and 6) training, exercises, and theater security cooperation activities. On September 30, 2008, President Bush signed into law H.R. 2638, the Consolidated Security, Disaster Assistance, and Continuing Appropriations Act, 2009 (P.L. 110-329). Under this legislation, which included defense appropriations, AFRICOM received $53 million less than what was requested. DOD officials suggest some of the items trimmed from the budget were restored following negotiations with the relevant committees, although the command lost some requested funding because of across-the- board cuts to the operations and maintenance account [38]. The identified cuts targeted the proposed regional offices, the TSOC, and DOD salaries for interagency personnel [39]. While the AFRICOM reduction is not as steep as was proposed in the House Defense Appropriations Subcommittee version of the bill, and the joint explanatory statement accompanying the final legislation expressed support for AFRICOM, the statement also insisted that the State Department and USAID should "play a more important role in this new organization supported with the appropriate manpower and funding required."

DOD's defense budget request for FY2010 includes approximately $278 million for AFRICOM [40]. Among the items identified for directed funding are 1) a new program of record, Air and Maritime Sector Development (AMSD); 2) an expansion of Operation Objective Voice (OOV; see below); 3) Standing Joint Force Headquarters (SJFHQ); 4) strategic communications; 5) satellite communications; 6) additional manpower (16 billets) for AFRICOM's Special Operations Command and an another 125 billets (55 military and 70 civilian billets for the SJFHQ, OSCs, and the command's Joint Operations Center).

The request reflects an increase in civilian pay for the command from an estimated $49 million in FY2009 to $74 million in FY20 10. It also includes funding for four new Offices of Security Cooperation in Cameroon, Chad, Libya, and Rwanda, and expansion of existing offices in Kenya, Liberia, and Morocco. The Department's military construction request includes $41.8 million for Camp Lemonier in Djibouti [41]. CJTF-HOA operations are classified as Overseas Contingency Operations and are funded separately from other AFRICOM activities [42].

To date they have been largely funded through emergency supplemental appropriations.

AFRICOM received approximately $30 million in FY2009 for operational airlift support, including $17.5 million for the 17th Air Force for military airlift and $12.5 million for TRANCOM to contract staff travel. AFRICOM leadership and staff have reported challenges posed by the routing and scheduling of commercial airlines traveling on the continent. DOD's FY2010 budget request includes $75 million for airlift, in addition to a C-37 that will be dedicated to AFRICOM in FY2011 and $100 million for a C-40, to be delivered in FY2012.

U.S. Strategic Interests in Africa

Issues on the African continent have not historically been identified as strategic priorities for the U.S. military, and U.S. military engagement in Africa has been sporadic [43]. According to one defense analyst, "during the Cold War, United States foreign policy toward Sub-Saharan Africa had little to do with Africa" [44].

Africa and the Unified Command Plan

Africa was not included in the U.S. military command structure until 1952, when several North African countries, including Libya, were added to the responsibilities of U.S. European Command because of their historic relationship with Europe. The rest of the continent remained outside the responsibility of any command until 1960, when Cold War concerns over Soviet influence in newly independent African countries led the Department of Defense to include Sub-Saharan Africa in the Atlantic Command (LANTCOM), leaving North Africa in EUCOM. The Unified Command Plan was revised again in 1962 by President John F. Kennedy, and responsibility for Sub-Saharan Africa was transferred to a newly-created Strike Command (STRICOM), which was responsible for operations in the Middle East, Sub-Saharan Africa, and South Asia. STRICOM was redesignated as Readiness Command (REDCOM) in 1971, and its responsibility for Africa was dissolved, leaving Sub-Saharan Africa out of the combatant command structure until 1983. Under the Reagan Administration, U.S. military involvement in Africa was largely dominated by Cold War priorities, and the Administration's "containment" policy led DOD to divide responsibility for Africa into its configuration among three geographic commands.

After the fall of the Soviet Union, many U.S. policymakers considered the U.S. military's role and responsibilities on the continent to be minimal. In 1995, the Department of Defense outlined its view of Africa in its U.S. Security Strategy for Sub- Saharan Africa, asserting that "ultimately we see very little traditional strategic interest in Africa" [45]. In 1998, following terrorist attacks on two U.S. embassies in East Africa, the United States conducted a retaliatory attack against a pharmaceutical factory in Khartoum, Sudan that Clinton Administration officials initially contended was producing precursors for chemical weapons for al Qaeda. The embassy bombings, and the retaliatory strike against Sudan, are considered by many analysts to be a turning point in U.S. strategic policy toward the region.

Current U.S. National Security Strategy toward Africa

The Bush Administration's National Security Strategy of 2002 reflected a need for a more focused strategic approach toward the African continent: "In Africa, promise and opportunity sit side by side with disease, war, and desperate poverty. This threatens both a core value of the United States—preserving human dignity—and our strategic priority—combating global terror." To address these challenges, the document asserted that U.S. security strategy must focus on building indigenous security and intelligence capabilities through bilateral engagement and "coalitions of the willing." [46]. The most recent National Security Strategy, issued in 2006, goes further, identifying Africa as "a high priority" and "recogniz(ing) that our security depends upon partnering with Africans to strengthen fragile and failing states and bring ungoverned areas under the control of effective democracies." [47].

The establishment of the new Africa Command reflects an evolution in policymakers' perceptions of U.S. strategic interests in Africa. In 2004 an advisory panel of Africa experts authorized by Congress to propose new policy initiatives identified five factors that have shaped increased U.S. interest in Africa in the past decade: oil, global trade, armed conflicts, terror, and HIV/AIDS [48]. They suggested that these factors had led to a "conceptual shift to a strategic view of Africa" [49].

Oil and Global Trade

The United States has sought to increase its economic relations with Sub-Saharan Africa, and trade between the United States and Africa has tripled since 1990. In 2000, the Clinton Administration introduced a comprehensive

U.S. trade and investment policy for the continent in the African Growth and Opportunity Act (AGOA; Title I, P.L. 106-200). AGOA has been amended by Congress on several occasions, most recently in 2006. Natural resources, particularly energy resources, dominate the products imported from Africa under AGOA. Africa now supplies the United States with roughly the same amount of crude oil as the Middle East [50].

Nigeria is Africa's largest supplier of oil, and is the fifth largest global supplier of oil to the United States. Instability in the country's Niger Delta region has reduced output periodically by over 25%. World oil prices have been affected by Nigerian political developments and by periodic attacks on pipelines and other oil facilities in the Delta. President Bush announced in his 2006 State of the Union Address his intention to "to replace more than 75 percent of our oil imports from the Middle East by 2025," [51] echoing a commitment made in 2002 "to strengthen [U.S.] energy security and the shared prosperity of the global economy by working with our allies, trading partners, and energy producers to expand the sources and types of global energy supplied, especially in the Western Hemisphere, Africa, Central Asia, and the Caspian region." [52]. A senior DOD official reportedly commented in 2003 that "a key mission for U.S. forces (in Africa) would be to ensure that Nigeria's oil fields... are secure" [53]. In spite of conflict in the Niger Delta and other oil producing areas, the potential for deep water drilling in the Gulf of Guinea is high, and analysts have estimated that Africa may supply as much as 25% of all U.S. oil imports by 2015 [54].

Maritime Security

Africa's coastlines, particularly along the Gulf of Guinea, the Gulf of Aden, and the west Indian Ocean, have been highly susceptible to illegal fishing, illegal trafficking, and piracy in recent years [55]. The inability of African governments to adequately police the region's waters has allowed criminal elements to smuggle people, drugs, and weapons and dump hazardous waste, and has opened maritime commerce and off-shore oil production facilities to the threat of piracy and sabotage. The growing problem of narcotics trafficking in West Africa, estimated by the U.N. Office on Drugs and Crime (UNODC) to be a transit point for approximately 27% of all cocaine annually consumed in Europe, has become an area of increasing concern to policymakers. In 2005, the Bush Administration introduced its National Strategy for Maritime Security, identifying the freedom of the seas and the facilitation and defense of commerce as top national priorities and indicating plans to fund border and coastal security initiatives with African countries [56].

The United States government, represented by members of EUCOM, U.S. Naval Forces Europe, the State Department, and the Africa Center for Strategic Studies (ACSS), has engaged its West African partners in a number of ministerial conferences on maritime security, and is currently conducting several activities to increase the capability of African navies to monitor and enforce maritime laws. The U.S. Navy has increased its operations in the Gulf of Guinea to enhance security in the region, although those operations have been sporadic [57]. Through its Global Fleet Stations (GFS) concept, the Navy has committed itself to more persistent, longer-term engagement (see information on the African Partnership Station in "Security Assistance" below). In the waters off the coast of East Africa, the Combined JointTask Force - Horn of Africa (CJTFHOA) is working with the Navy and with coalition partners in CENTCOM's Coalition Task Force 151 (CTF- 151), which conducts maritime security operations to protect shipping routes in the Gulf of Aden, Gulf of Oman, the Arabian Sea, Red Sea, and the Indian Ocean [58]. Coalition and U.S. naval forces have had numerous engagements with pirates in these waters.

Armed Conflicts

Political conflict and instability in parts of Africa have caused human suffering on a massive scale and undermined economic, social, and political development [59]. Although the number of conflicts in Africa has decreased in recent years, the continent is home to a majority of the United Nations' peace operations, with seven missions currently underway [60]. Four African countries, Ghana, Ethiopia, Nigeria, and South Africa have consistently ranked in the top 10 troop contributing countries to U.N. peacekeeping operations in recent years. African militaries also contribute troops to peace operations conducted by the African Union and regional organizations like ECOWAS. Despite a willingness to participate in these operations, many African militaries lack the command and control, training, equipment, and logistics capability to effectively participate in such efforts. Instability in Africa has demanded substantial humanitarian and defense resources from the international community, and the United States and other donor countries have acknowledged the utility and potential cost-effectiveness of assisting African forces to enhance their capabilities to participate in these operations. In 2004, the G8 introduced the Global Peace Operations Initiative (GPOI), a five-year multilateral program to train 75,000 troops, a majority of them African, by 2010 [61].

Violent Extremism

U.S. security policy has been driven largely, in recent years, by counter-terrorism efforts, which the Bush Administration identified as a top national security priority [62]. Terrorist attacks on the U.S. embassies in Dar es Salaam, Tanzania and Nairobi, Kenya in 1998, on targets in Mombasa, Kenya in 2002 and more recently in Algeria, Mauritania, Morocco, and Somalia have highlighted the threat of violent extremism in the region. In a March 2009 Senate Armed Services Committee hearing on national security threats, Director of National Intelligence Dennis Blair expressed concern over Al Qaeda in the Islamic Maghreb (AQIM) and the increasing capabilities of terrorist groups in East Africa [63]. U.S. officials have also warned that recruitment and support networks continue to operate in Africa, facilitating the activities of foreign fighters in Iraq, Afghanistan, and Pakistan [64]. DOD officials have emphasized the need to work with African governments to counteract the threat, claiming "Africa has been, is now, and will be into the foreseeable future ripe for terrorists and acts of terrorism" [65]. Of primary concern to policy makers is the possible challenge posed by "ungoverned spaces," defined as "physical or non-physical area(s) where there is an absence of state capacity or political will to exercise control" [66]. The Bush Administration linked these areas indirectly to terrorist threats, asserting:

> Regional conflicts can arise from a wide variety of causes, including poor governance, external aggression, competing claims, internal revolt, tribal rivalries, and ethnic or religious hatreds. If left unaddressed, however, these different causes lead to the same ends: failed states, humanitarian disasters, and ungoverned areas that can become safe havens for terrorists [67].

In addition to failed states providing a potential "safe haven" for terrorists, there is evidence to suggest terrorist groups may have profited from the collapse of state administrative and security institutions in Sierra Leone and Liberia in the 1990s by trafficking gemstones during Sierra Leone's civil war. Reports suggest that al Qaeda used the proceeds from its "conflict diamond" trade as a funding source for its operations [68]. State Department officials have identified failed states such as these as an "acute risk" to U.S. national security [69].

HIV/AIDS

According to the United Nations, there were over 22 million HIV-positive Africans in 2007, representing 67% of infected persons worldwide [70]. HIV/AIDS is the leading cause of death on the continent and was identified by former Secretary of State Colin Powell as "the greatest threat of mankind today" [71]. The rate of infection in some African security forces is believed to be high, reportedly between 40%-60% in the case of one southern African country, for example, raising concerns that those forces may be unable to deploy when needed [72]. The Bush Administration and Congress placed priority on efforts to combat HIV/AIDS, committing over $48 billion through the President's Emergency Plan for AIDS Relief (PEPFAR). Twelve of PEPFAR's 15 focus countries are in Africa [73]. As part of the Administration's efforts, DOD has established the DOD HIV/AIDS Prevention Program (DHAPP) with African armed forces, which is administered by the Naval Health Research Center in San Diego. DHAPP supports programs in 39 countries, many of which do not receive PEPFAR funds.

U.S. Military Assistance and Security Cooperation in Africa: An Expanding Role

The Department of Defense conducts a wide variety of activities in Africa in support of U.S. national interests. Operational activities may include, but are not limited to, humanitarian relief, [74] peacekeeping, counter-narcotics, sanctions enforcement, demining, non-combatant evacuations (NEOs), and maritime interdiction operations (MIOs).

In addition to traditional contingency operations [75], the U.S. military implements a number of efforts aimed at increasing the capabilities of African militaries to provide security and stability for their own countries and the region as a whole. Several of these DOD-implemented initiatives are part of foreign military assistance programs funded by the State Department that "help to promote the principles of democracy, respect for human rights, and the rule of law." [76]. In addition to providing funding, the State Department gives overall guidance and direction for the programs. The United States military also occasionally provides advisors to peacekeeping missions on the continent; U.S. military advisors from CJTF-HOA have assisted peacekeepers deployed to Sudan and Somalia. U.S. forces routinely conduct a variety of bilateral and multilateral joint exercises with African militaries through such programs as Joint Combined Exchange Training (JCET). U.S. forces also conduct joint exercises as part of disaster assistance and maritime security training.

The Africa Center for Strategic Studies (ACSS) was created in 1999 as one of DOD's five regional centers for strategic studies. It conducts a variety of academic activities for African, American, and European military and civilian officials aimed promoting good governance and democratic values, countering ideological support of terrorism, and fostering regional collaboration and cooperation in the African defense and security sectors. ACSS, which is based in Washington, DC, opened an annex at the U.S. embassy in Ethiopia in 2006 and is planning future annexes elsewhere on the continent [77]. DOD initiated another multi-nation forum, the Africa Clearinghouse, in 2004 under EUCOM. The Africa Clearinghouse, modeled after EUCOM Clearinghouses for Southeast Europe and the South Caucasus, provides a venue for the United States to coordinate its actions with other nations involved in security cooperation in Africa to maximize limited resources, synchronize security assistance, and avoid duplication of efforts.

The United States sells military equipment to African governments through the Foreign Military Sales (FMS) program, implemented by the U.S. Defense Security Cooperation Agency (DSCA) [78].

The U.S. government also provides loans (the United States waives repayment of these loans for African countries) to foreign governments to finance the purchase of such equipment through the Foreign Military Financing (FMF) program. Equipment is also provided to select African countries through the African Coastal and Border Security Program (ACBSP) and the Excess Defense Articles (EDA) program, and through special DOD authorities.

U.S. counter-terrorism strategy on the continent is addressed through a number of these initiatives, but U.S. counter-terrorism efforts may also include, at one end of the spectrum, programs to address the root causes of terrorism, and, at the other end, military operations to destroy terrorist targets through military strikes.

The United States is placing increasing emphasis on Information Operations (IO) in Africa, which use information to improve the security environment and counter extremist ideology through military information support teams deployed to U.S. embassies. IO activities in Africa have included website initiatives such as Maghrebia.com and AFRICOM's Operation Objective Voice (OOV), an interagency effort to counter extremist messaging [79]. Some question whether activities such as these should be a part of DOD's mandate, or whether they might be more appropriately managed by other U.S. agencies.

DOD officials argue that AFRICOM not only allows the U.S. military to better coordinate these operations and programs, but that it also allows DOD to better coordinate with other U.S. agencies, like the State Department, USAID, the Department of Justice, the Central Intelligence Agency, the Federal Bureau of Investigations and others, as well as with other governments, like those of Britain and France, which are also providing training and assistance for African security forces. DOD suggests that Africa Command builds on the experiences of the U.S. military's only forward presence in the region, Combined Joint Task Force—Horn of Africa (CJTF-HOA) in Djibouti.

Combined Joint Task Force: Horn of Africa (CJTF-HOA)

In October 2002, the United States Central Command (CENTCOM) developed a joint task force to focus on "detecting, disrupting and ultimately defeating transnational terrorist groups operating in the region," and to provide a forward presence in the region [80].

Under AFRICOM, the task force's mission has evolved to more broadly reflect a strategy of "cooperative conflict prevention." Between 1,500 and 2,500 short-term rotational U.S. military and civilian personnel make up CJTF-HOA, which covers the land and airspace in Kenya, Somalia, Sudan, Seychelles, Ethiopia, Eritrea, Djibouti, and Yemen, as well as the coastal waters of the Red Sea, the Gulf of Aden, and the Indian Ocean.

CJTF personnel train the region's security forces in counter-terrorism and other areas of military professionalization, collect intelligence, serve as advisors to peace operations, and oversee and support humanitarian assistance efforts. Although U.S. Central Command maintains primary responsibility for naval operations against pirates in the waters off the Horn of Africa, CJTF-HOA personnel provide security assistance to several regional maritime security forces, few of which have "blue water capacity." The Task Force has provided military assistance and training to Ugandan military forces deployed in support of the African Union Peacekeeping Mission in Somalia (AMISOM).

As part of this effort, CJTF-HOA worked with non-governmental organizations to provide medical supplies to the Ugandan forces for assistance to the people of Mogadishu. CJTF-HOA has supported several humanitarian missions, including the airlift of humanitarian assistance supplies to Ethiopia and Northern Kenya. CJTF-HOA also conducts civilian-military operations throughout East Africa as part of an effort to "win hearts and minds" [81] and enhance the "long-term stability of the region." [82].

These civil-military operations include digging wells and building and repairing schools, hospitals, and roads, and were part of a broader CENTCOM mission to "counter the re-emergence of transnational terrorism." [83]. Some observers question whether these activities might be more appropriately coordinated by a civilian agency or non-governmental organization than by the U.S. military. AFRICOM officials have suggested that the scope of these activities is being reexamined.

Security Assistance

Building partnership capacity is a key goal of U.S. military strategy in Africa and is consequently a key mandate for AFRICOM. At present, military experts believe that no African nation poses a direct threat to the United States or is expected to; consequently Africa Command is expected to focus less on preparing U.S. forces for major combat in the AOR. Instead, the command will concentrate much of its energies and resources on training and assistance to professionalize local militaries so that they can better ensure stability and security on the continent.

As one DOD official has asserted, "its principle mission will be in the area of security cooperation and building partnership capability. It will not be in warfighting." [84]. Officials stress that U.S. training programs aim to encourage respect for human rights and for civilian authority, key shortcomings for some African security forces.

The U.S. government provides security assistance to African militaries through both bilateral and multilateral initiatives. During the 1990s, the United States provided military training through several programs, including the African Crisis Response Initiative (ACRI), the Enhanced International Peacekeeping Capabilities (EIPC) program, the African Regional Peace-keeping Program (ARP), and International Military Education and Training (IMET). Some of this training has been provided by the U.S. Army 3rd and 10th Special Forces Groups, which have worked with African militaries since 1990. Training has also been provided by contractors. Under the National Guard State Partnership Program (SPP), U.S. states' and territories' National

Guard units have paired with several African countries to conduct a variety of security cooperation activities [85]. The U.S. military has worked with the continent's regional security organizations, including the African Union (AU) and the Economic Community of West African States (ECOWAS). U.S. military efforts also aim to support the development of the African Union's African Standby Force (ASF), a multinational peacekeeping force composed of regional brigades organized by the continent's Regional Economic Communities [86].

The AU aims for the Force to be operational by 2010 with a standby capacity of 15,000 to 20,000 peacekeepers. The ASF and its regional brigades are not intended to be standing forces, but will instead draw from pre-identified forces of member states. AFRICOM continues to conduct annual training exercises begun under EUCOM, such African Endeavor, a communications and interoperability exercise that will include 23 African nations in 2009. U.S. military assistance also includes efforts to improve information sharing networks between African countries through programs such as the Multinational Information Sharing Initiative, which donor and aid organizations can in turn use to warn of and be warned of possible crises. AFRICOM also supports U.S. security sector reform initiatives in post-conflict countries like Liberia.

Several of the other major current bilateral and multilateral security assistance programs implemented by DOD in Africa are listed below (the list is not inclusive) [87]. These programs fall under the mission of Africa Command.

African Partnership Station (APS)

In October 2007, U.S. Naval Forces Europe launched a new initiative, the African Partnership Station (APS). Under the initiative, a navy ship, the USS Fort McHenry, was deployed to the Gulf of Guinea from fall 2007 to spring 2008 to serve as a continuing sea base of operations and a "floating schoolhouse" from which to provide assistance and training to the Gulf nations [88]. Training focused on maritime domain awareness and law enforcement, port facilities management and security, seamanship/navigation, search and rescue, leadership, logistics, civil engineering, humanitarian assistance and disaster response. Several other Navy and Coast Guard vessels have subsequently deployed to the region under the APS banner. Several European partners, NGOs, and U.S. government agencies, including the Coast Guard and the National Oceanographic and Atmospheric Administration (NOAA), have partnered with the Navy to use the Station, which is considered by the

Navy to be a "delivery vehicle for interagency, international, and NGO assistance" to West, Central, and East Africa, for their own training and development initiatives [89]. Humanitarian outreach activities have included Project Handclasp and Project Hope. The APS vessels have had a minimal footprint onshore, and have conducted repeat visits to ports along the African coast. The cost for APS in FY20 10 is estimated at $10.5 million for deployments in West and Central Africa and $9.96 million for East Africa [90].

Operation Enduring Freedom: Trans Sahara (OEF-TS)/Trans Sahara Counter- Terrorism Partnership (TSCTP)

In 2002, the Department of State launched the Pan-Sahel Initiative (PSI) program to increase border security and counter-terrorism capacities of four West African nations: Mali, Chad, Niger, and Mauritania. In 2005, the Bush Administration announced a "follow-on" interagency program to PSI. According to the State Department, the Trans Sahara Counter-Terrorism Partnership (formerly Initiative) is "aimed at defeating terrorist organizations by strengthening regional counterterrorism capabilities, enhancing and institutionalizing cooperation among the region's security forces, promoting democratic governance, discrediting terrorist ideology, and reinforcing bilateral military ties with the United States." [91]. Under the American military component, Operation Enduring Freedom - Trans Sahara, which AFRICOM took responsibility for in fall 2008, U.S. forces work with their African counterparts from Algeria, Burkina Faso, Chad, Libya, Mali, Mauritania, Morocco, Niger, Nigeria, Senegal, and Tunisia to improve intelligence, command and control, logistics, and border control, and to execute joint operations against terrorist groups [92]. U.S. and African forces have conducted joint exercises such as Exercise Flintlock to improve security partnerships initiated under PSI and TSCTP.

These military efforts are designed to support complimentary development activities led by the State Department and USAID. To counter the recruitment efforts of terrorist groups, for example, USAID supports job creation initiatives for disadvantaged youth. Young people are a key demographic in Africa, where high unemployment rates and scarce education opportunities compound the challenges posed by a growing "youth bulge." Such programs are coordinated with the efforts of U.S. military personnel working in the region. The United States allocated over $353 million for TSCTP from FY2005 through FY2008. The State Department's East Africa Regional

Security Initiative (EARSI), a smaller program, has been designed to build upon the best practices of TSCTP.

International Military Education and Training (IMET)

In 1949 the U.S. government began providing training to foreign militaries under the Military Assistance Training Program (MAP) and through Foreign Military Sales (FMS), which allows countries to pay for their own training. MAP was succeeded in 1976 by IMET, which provides training at U.S. military schools and other training assistance for foreign military personnel on a grant basis through funding from the Department of State. A subset of IMET training, Expanded IMET (E-IMET), provides courses on defense management, civil-military relations, law enforcement cooperation, and military justice for military as well as civilian personnel. The State Department also provides training through its Foreign Military Financing (FMF) program. Sub- Saharan African countries received approximately $13.8 million in IMET assistance in FY2008 and FY2009; $16 million has been requested for FY2010.

The African Contingency Operations Training and Assistance Program (ACOTA)/ Global Peace Operations Initiative (GPOI)

In 1996, the Clinton Administration proposed the creation of an African Crisis Response Force (ACRF), an African standby force that would be trained and equipped by the United States and other donor nations. The initiative was not well received on the continent, and was later reintroduced as the African Crisis Response Initiative (ACRI), a bilateral training program designed to improve the capabilities of individual African countries' militaries to participate in multilateral peacekeeping operations. ACOTA, which replaced ACRI in 2002, aims to upgrade the peace-enforcement capabilities of African militaries.

ACOTA provides Peace Support Operations training, including light infantry and small unit tactics, and focuses on training African troops who can in turn train other African units. In 2004, ACOTA became a part of GPOI. GPOI attempts to address some of the factors limiting African militaries' ability to contribute to peace operations by conducting a variety of programs, events, and activities oriented on peacekeeping capacity building. Among these programs is an effort to foster an international transport and logistics support system for African and other region's forces.

The United States coordinates its peacekeeping training and assistance programs with other G8 countries through a G8 Africa Clearinghouse. While the State Department is the executive agent of GPOI and ACOTA, the DOD provides small military teams for special mentoring assistance to ACOTA training events.

According to the State Department, over 60,000 peacekeepers from Benin, Botswana, Burkina Faso, Burundi, Cameroon, Cote d'Ivoire, Ethiopia, Gabon, Ghana, Kenya, Malawi, Mali, Mauritania, Mozambique, Namibia, Niger, Nigeria, Rwanda, Senegal, South Africa, Tanzania, Uganda, and Zambia have received ACOTA training since the program's inception [93]. Over $110 million has been obligated for GPOI in FY2009, with $49 million allocated for ACOTA and over $9 million for support to the AU and ECOWAS headquarters. The Obama Administration has requested $96.8 million for GPOI for FY2010 [94].

REGIONAL PERSPECTIVES

U.S. reaction to the creation of a new command for Africa has been largely positive, although concerns have been raised [95]. In Africa, on the other hand, perceptions of the new command are more mixed. There has been considerable apprehension over U.S. motivations for creating AFRICOM, and some Africans worry that the move represents a neo-colonial effort to dominate the region militarily. U.S. military efforts on the continent have been seen as episodic, leading some to question a more sustained focus from DOD now. Reports of U.S. air strikes in Somalia in recent years and U.S. support for Ethiopia's military intervention there have added to those concerns. Many view U.S. counter-terrorism efforts in Africa with skepticism, and there appears to be a widespread belief that the new command's primary goals will be to hunt terrorists and to secure U.S. access to African oil [96]. U.S. foreign policy analysts have focused increased attention on China's role in Africa in recent years, and such attention has led some to question whether an Africa Command might be part of a new contest for influence on the continent [97].

Among several African governments and militaries, on the other hand, AFRICOM has been received with cautious optimism [98]. They view increased American attention to the continent's problems as a positive move, potentially bringing increased resources, training, and assistance. U.S. foreign military assistance has increased in recent years, and military training programs in Africa have steadily been on the rise.

DOD and State Department officials continue to consult with African nations to discuss their plans for the command. Those involved in the consultations have stressed that the goal of the visits has been to solicit African views and explain the rationale behind AFRICOM's creation, rather than to find a suitable location for its headquarters. In April 2007, senior officials visited Nigeria, South Africa, Kenya, Ethiopia, Ghana and Senegal. Following their visit, one DOD official noted that despite some initial "misconceptions," they had not encountered "any specific resistance to the idea" [99]. In June 2007, they visited Algeria, Morocco, Libya, Egypt, and Djibouti, and held discussions with African Union officials. The delegation also held meetings with 40 foreign defense attachés serving in Paris. African officials reportedly gave "positive feedback about the design and mission of AFRICOM" and advised the delegation that DOD should consider how AFRICOM could complement the AU's regional security structure [100]. In September 2007, DOD hosted representatives from the African Union, African regional security organizations, and over 35 African governments in Virginia to further explain its plans for the command and to solicit input from attendees; a similar event was held in April 2008. Analysts suggest U.S. officials should continue to closely consult with these governments to ensure that AFRICOM reflects a mutual exchange of interests and is seen to foster a closer alliance rather than serving as an avenue for the U.S. to dictate policy to African governments.

AFRICOM's commander has acknowledged the need for his staff to continue their public relations campaign to allay concerns [101]. In October 2007, members of the Pan-African Parliament, the legislative body of the African Union, voted in favor of a motion to "prevail upon all African Governments through the African Union (AU) not to accede to the United States of America's Government's request to host AFRICOM anywhere in the African continent." [102]. West African military chiefs, following a November 2007 conference in Liberia, issued a cautious response to U.S. government plans, saying that AFRICOM "had not been fully understood" by African countries and requesting "further sensitization by the United States authorities at the highest political level." ECOWAS's Commissioner for Political Affairs, Peace, and Security did suggest that "everybody welcomes and supports the idea, but we want that direction to come from the heads of state." [103].

Several African heads of state issued preliminary statements about their views on the command. Some advised DOD to consider how AFRICOM could complement the AU's regional security structure. Nigerian President Umaru Yar'Adua, during his December 2007 visit to Washington, D.C., commented, "We shall partner with AFRICOM to assist not only Nigeria, but also the African continent to actualize its peace and security initiative, which is an initiative to help standby forces of brigade-size in each of the regional economic groupings within the African continent." [104]. Yar'Adua's statements were criticized by several Nigerian opposition parties and civil society organizations. In response, Nigeria's Minister of Foreign Affairs remarked, "Nigeria's position on AFRICOM remains that African governments have the sovereign responsibility for the maintenance of peace and security on the continent ... President Yar'Adua's statement on the proposed AFRICOM is consistent with Nigeria's well-known position on the necessity for Africa to avail itself of opportunities for enhanced capacity for the promotion of peace and security in Africa." [105]. During President Bush's second official visit to Africa in February 2008, Ghana's President John Kufour announced, "I am happy, one, for the President dispelling any notion that the United States of America is intending to build military bases on the continent of Africa. I believe the explanation the President has given should put fade to the speculation, so that the relationship between us and the United States will grow stronger and with mutual respect." [106]. Liberia's President Ellen Johnson-Sirleaf has been vocal in her support from AFRICOM, and has offered to host its headquarters.

As AFRICOM has assumed ongoing security engagement operations from EUCOM and CENTCOM and initiated new programs, its officials have stressed the need for improved strategic communications efforts to increase understanding of the command among African governments and their people. In October 2008, the South African government, initially one of the most vocal on the continent in expressing concerns about the new command, welcomed the USS Theodore Roosevelt, the first U.S. carrier to visit the country since the end of apartheid. The new President of South Africa, Jacob Zuma, has yet to publicly express his views on AFRICOM.

Congressional Interest and Oversight Issues

As noted above, AFRICOM continues to face myriad challenges, both in its establishment and its operation. Some of these challenges may be issues for Congress. Several Members of Congress expressed interest in the creation of an Africa Command prior to the Bush Administration decision. In 2006, Senator Russ Feingold introduced S.Amdt. 4527 to the FY2007 National Defense Authorization bill (S. 2766) requiring a feasibility study for the establishment of a new command for Africa. S. 2766 passed the Senate in June 2006. In December 2007, Representative Ileana Ros-Lehtinen introduced

H.Res. 897, recognizing the strategic importance of the African continent and welcoming the establishment of AFRICOM. Senator James Inhofe introduced similar legislation, S.Res. 480, in March 2008. These resolutions also urge the Departments of Defense and State, as well as USAID, to consult with African partners to address concerns regarding the command's mandate. The Africa Subcommittees of the Senate Foreign Relations Committee and the House Committee on Foreign Affairs both held hearings on AFRICOM in August 2007. Following General Ward's confirmation as commander, the House Armed Services Committee held a hearing to discuss the command in November 2007. He later testified in February and March 2008 before the Senate and House Armed Services Committees, respectively. General Ward testified before the 111th Congress in February 2009, before the Senate Armed Services Committee, and in March 2009, before the House Armed Services Committee and the House Appropriations Defense Subcommittee.

Congress has addressed issues associated with the command's development in report language accompanying several authorization and appropriations bills. The Senate Armed Services Committee expressed its support for AFRICOM in S.Rept. 110-77, which accompanied S. 1547, the National Defense Authorization Act, 2008. The report did, however, raise questions regarding authorities needed to stand up and staff the command; authorities and funding mechanisms for interagency staff; location; planned staffing levels; and anticipated costs. The committee repeated its support in S.Rept. 110-335, which accompanied S. 3001, the National Defense Authorization Act, 2009, but expressed concern that other U.S. government agencies may not have the resources to support the command's "whole of government" approach.

In S.Rept. 111-135, accompanying S. 1390, the National Defense Authorization Act, 2010, the committee expressed support for the persistent regional engagement activities conducted by AFRICOM's Combined Joint Task Force– Horn of Africa, but requested clarification from DOD on the future role of the Task Force on the continent. The House Armed Services Committee raised questions regarding AFRICOM's mission in H.Rept. 110-652, which accompanied H.R. 5658, the Duncan Hunter National Defense Authorization Act, 2009. The Senate Appropriations Committee also noted its concern regarding unanswered questions surrounding the command's mission in S.Rept. 110-85 accompanying H.R. 2642, the Military Construction and Veterans Affairs and Related Agencies Appropriations Act, 2008, and in the conference report to H.R. 1585, the National Defense Authorization Act, 2008 (H.Rept. 110-477). Such concerns were repeated in S.Rept. 110-428, which accompanied S. 3301, the Military Construction and Veterans Affairs and Related Agencies Appropriations Act, 2009. H.Rept. 110-775, accompanying the House version of that legislation, H.R. 6599, raised specific concern with unanswered questions related to the permanent location of AFRICOM's headquarters. Reference to AFRICOM in the joint explanatory statement accompanying H.R. 2638, the Consolidated Security, Disaster Assistance, and Continuing Appropriations Act, 2009 (P.L. 110-329), has been discussed above (see "Cost").

AFRICOM's mandate has also been considered by Congress within the broader context of DOD's role in U.S. foreign affairs. During the 110th Congress, AFRICOM was the focus of a series of hearings by the House Committee on Oversight and Government Reform's Subcommittee on National Security and Foreign Affairs. The command was discussed by the Senate Foreign Relations Committee in several hearings, including one entitled "Implementing Smart Power: Setting an Agenda for National Security Reform" in April 2008 and another in July 2008 entitled "Defining the Military's Role Toward Foreign Policy." During an April 2008 hearing on Building Partnership Capacity, the Secretaries of State and Defense both addressed AFRICOM's unique interagency approach in testimony before the House Armed Services Committee. In June 2008, the command was also addressed in a House Foreign Affairs Committee hearing entitled "Foreign Assistance Reform: Rebuilding U.S. Civilian Development and Diplomatic Capacity in the 21st Century." The House Armed Services Committee has commissioned a Panel on Roles and Missions of not only the various military branches, but also of the various civilian agencies involved in protecting American security. Among its initial findings was the notion that shortcomings in the interagency process have led the U.S. military to take on missions that are not part of its core responsibilities. The FY2008 National Defense Authorization Act required the military to examine its core competencies, which may ultimately have implications for AFRICOM. Some observers have cautioned that AFRICOM could develop independent institutional imperatives that demand resources regardless of need, rather than reflecting genuine strategic interests.

Given that a large part of AFRICOM's mandate is to build the indigenous capacity of African defense forces, the ease with which the command can conduct security cooperation programs will be key to its success. DOD officials suggest that inefficiencies exist in the authorities through which funding is provided for the military's TSC activities [107]. Some military officials have argued that the applicable laws need simplification to allow the combatant commands greater flexibility to respond to emerging threats and opportunities. Others have raised concerns, though, that modifying the administrative authorities could interfere with the Department of State's diplomatic decisions or bilateral relationships. The U.S. military has faced other policy restrictions, including Article 98 restrictions, in its operations with some African governments and militaries [108]. At the same time, DOD is also concerned about possible gaps in servicemen protections for U.S. troops operating on the continent (see "Headquarters Location" above). The Government Accountability Office has noted in testimony to Congress that "uncertainties related to AFRICOM's presence hinder DOD's ability to estimate future funding requirements for AFRICOM and raises questions about whether DOD's concept of developing enduring relationships on the continent can be achieved."

The establishment of a new unified command requires both financial and human resources, although some of those have been redirected from the other commands. Military resources have been stretched by major theater operations in Iraq and Afghanistan, making troop readiness and costs associated with standing up a new command a critical issue for Congress [109]. Staffing the command at the interagency level may also require additional resources from Congress—some officials at the State Department and USAID have expressed concern about their departments' inability to provide the number of civilian staff requested by the command, and that concern that has been echoed by DOD [110]. The State Department has requested funding to increase the number of diplomatic and development personnel at State and USAID to allow the agencies to focus greater effort on meeting national security goals. The Secretary of Defense has also advocated on behalf of the civilian agencies, emphasizing that the State Department is critically understaffed [111].

The development of AFRICOM's interagency staffing has been of particular interest to Congress. In the House Report to accompany H.R. 2082, the Intelligence Authorization Act of FY2008, the Permanent Select Committee on Intelligence expressed concern with interagency coordination on Africa, calling it "flawed" and suggesting that the intelligence community needed to realign its resources to "better understand the threats emanating from this region." DOD officials point out that there are no legally binding requirements for agencies to coordinate their activities, which could make AFRICOM's "pioneering" interagency process more challenging, should other agencies not have the resources to participate adequately [112]. Because the command's role is to support U.S. foreign policy objectives in Africa, close coordination with the State Department will be critical to the success of

AFRICOM. Some have suggested that because the State Department organizes its efforts bilaterally while DOD organizes regionally, that coordination may be challenging and may require some "internal bureaucratic changes" within the State Department [113].

Observers have expressed concern that U.S. military efforts on the continent must not be allowed to overshadow U.S. diplomatic objectives. A 2006 Senate Foreign Affairs Committee Report found that

> As a result of inadequate funding for civilian programs... U.S. defense agencies are increasingly being granted authority and funding to fill perceived gaps. Such bleeding of civilian responsibilities overseas from civilian to military agencies risks weakening the Secretary of State's primacy in setting the agenda for U.S. relations with foreign countries and the Secretary of Defense's focus on war fighting [114].

Senator Feingold, in several speeches before the Senate, has expressed his support for the Africa Command, but has cautioned that it must "contribute to, not define, the U.S. Government's overall strategy and objectives for the continent." [115]. Likewise, Senator Richard Lugar has suggested that AFRICOM could help the U.S. military develop a "more sophisticated understanding of a region that is ever-changing and highly complex," but has also cautioned, "with greater expertise created within a new regional command, the hope is that there would be few disagreements between the two Departments on the appropriateness of security assistance to specific African nations. But undoubtedly, some differences of opinion will occur."[116]. As AFRICOM develops, Congress may exert its oversight authority to monitor the command's operations to ensure that they support, rather than guide, the United States' political, economic, and social objectives for the continent.

RELATED CRS REPORTS

CRS Report RL34455, *Organizing the U.S. Government for National Security: Overview of the Interagency Reform Debates,* by Catherine Dale, Nina M. Serafino, and Pat Towell.

CRS Report RL3 2773, *The Global Peace Operations Initiative: Background and Issues for Congress*, by Nina M. Serafino.

CRS Report RL32238, *Defense Transformation: Background and Oversight Issues for Congress,* by Ronald O'Rourke.

CRS Report R40528, *Piracy off the Horn of Africa*, by Lauren Ploch et al..

CRS Report RS22373, *Navy Role in Irregular Warfare and Counterterrorism: Background and Issues for Congress*, by Ronald O'Rourke.

CRS Report RL33769, *International Crises and Disasters: U.S. Humanitarian Assistance, Budget Trends, and Issues for Congress*, by Rhoda Margesson.

CRS Report RL34639, *The Department of Defense Role in Foreign Assistance: Background, Major Issues, and Options for Congress*, coordinated by Nina M. Serafino.

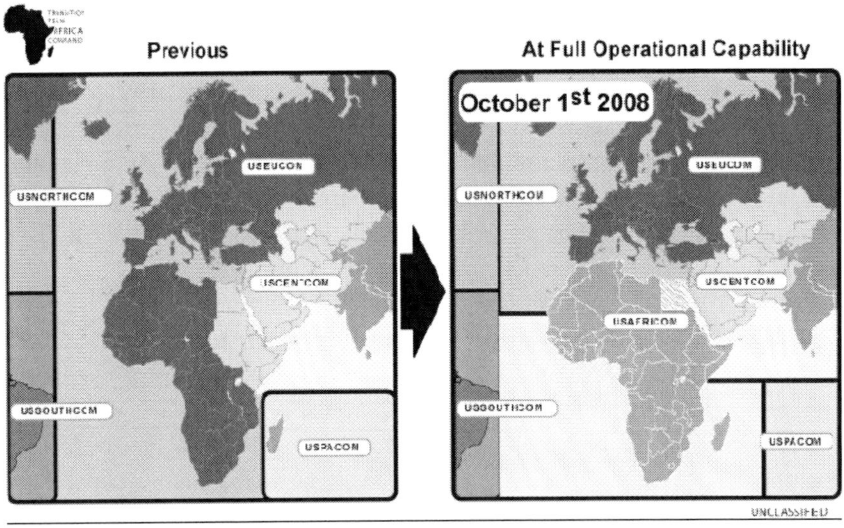

Source: Department of Defense, adapted by CRS.

Figure 1. Proposed Area of Responsibility for Africa Command.

APPENDIX A. HISTORY OF U.S. MILITARY INVOLVEMENT IN AFRICA

The United States maintained Wheelus Air Base near Tripoli, Libya from the 1940s until 1971 with an estimated 4,000 American personnel [117]. Wheelus served primarily as a bomber base for missions to Europe and as an Air Force training location, although U.S. forces from the base did provide emergency humanitarian assistance to earthquake and flood victims in Libya and Tunisia in the 1960s.

Africa was not included in the U.S. military command structure until 1952, when several North African countries, including Libya, were added to the responsibilities of U.S. European Command because of their historic relationship with Europe. The rest of the continent remained outside the responsibility of any command until 1960, when Cold War concerns over Soviet influence in newly independent African countries led DOD to include Sub-Saharan Africa in the Atlantic Command (LANTCOM), leaving North Africa in EUCOM. The Unified Command Plan was revised again in 1962 by President John F. Kennedy, and responsibility for Sub-Saharan Africa was transferred to a newly-created Strike Command (STRICOM), which was responsible for operations in the Middle East, Sub-Saharan Africa, and South Asia and located at McDill Air Force Base in Tampa, Florida. STRICOM was redesignated as Readiness Command (REDCOM) in 1971, and its responsibility for Africa was dissolved, leaving Sub-Saharan Africa out of the combatant command structure until 1983. Under the Reagan Administration, U.S. military involvement in Africa was largely dominated by Cold War priorities, and the Administration's "containment" policy led DOD to divide responsibility for Africa into its current configuration.

In the 1980s, the U.S. military was involved in repeated skirmishes with Libyan jets in territorial disputes over the Gulf of Sidra, and those engagements later escalated as Libya was implicated for supporting international terrorism. On April 15, 1986, the United States initiated air strikes against multiple military targets in Libya under the code name Operation El Dorado Canyon to "inflict damage to Qadhafi's capability to direct and control the export of international terrorism;" several civilian targets including the French Embassy in Tripoli were also inadvertently hit [118].

After the end of the Cold War, U.S. policy toward Africa was driven by President George H. W. Bush's vision of a "New World Order" [119] and later by President William J. Clinton's policy of "assertive multilateralism." [120] U.S. military involvement in Africa was dominated by the deployment of U.S. forces to Somalia to secure humanitarian operations, first in 1992 under the U.S.-led Unified Task Force (UNITAF), also known as Operation Restore Hope, and later under the United Nations Operation in Somalia (UNOSOM) II [121]. U.S. military efforts in Somalia were unprecedented on the continent—over 25,000 U.S. soldiers were deployed by President George H.W. Bush under UNITAF, which was led by CENTCOM and included forces from 24 other countries.

The number of U.S. troops was significantly reduced under President Clinton as operational responsibility was shifted from UNITAF to UNOSOM

II. In October 1993, U.S. Special Operations soldiers in the U.S.-led Task Force Ranger engaged Somali militia forces in the battle of Mogadishu, which ultimately resulted in the deaths of 18 American soldiers and hundreds of Somalis [122]. President Clinton ultimately ordered the withdrawal of U.S. forces from Somalia in March 1994, the same month that a limited U.S. deployment of 3,600 soldiers was dispatched to Central Africa to assist in humanitarian efforts for Rwandan refugees and to provide protection for humanitarian supplies in Rwanda [123].

In 1995, DOD outlined its view of Africa in its U.S. Security Strategy for Sub-Saharan Africa, asserting that "ultimately we see very little traditional strategic interest in Africa" [124]. While the U.S. military was deployed almost annually during the 1990s to conduct Non-Combatant Evacuation and Repatriation Operations (NEO) in African countries that had become politically unstable, other contingency operations [125] involving U.S. forces in Africa in latter half of the 1990s were limited. In 1998, following the attacks on two U.S. embassies in East Africa, the United States conducted retaliatory cruise missile attacks against a pharmaceutical factory in Khartoum, Sudan that Clinton Administration officials initially contended was producing precursors for chemical weapons for al Qaeda.

In 2003, the United States responded to calls to intervene in Liberia's civil war by deploying a U.S. Amphibious Ready Group (ARG) off the coast of Liberia to provide assistance to the ECOWAS mission in Liberia (ECOMIL) through Joint Task Force Liberia, under the command of EUCOM [126]. Out of an estimated 5,000 U.S. forces deployed to the area under Operation Sheltering Sky, only approximately 200 U.S. soldiers came ashore.

More recently, U.S. military personnel have provided training and logistical support for African peacekeepers in both Sudan and Somalia, and have provided counter-terrorism training to select African military units in the Sahel region. As discussed above, the U.S. Navy continues to conduct anti-piracy patrols off the coast of East Africa. According to media reports, the U.S. military has, in recent years, also engaged in air strikes against suspected terrorist targets in Somalia. AFRICOM officials have acknowledged that the command provided logistical and advisory support for a joint military operation between the armies of Uganda, the DRC, and Southern Sudan in December 2008 against the Ugandan insurgent group known as the Lord's Resistance Army [127].

Appendix B. Instances of the Use of U.S. Armed Forces in Africa, 1950-2008 [128]

1956 Egypt. A marine battalion evacuated U.S. nationals and other persons from Alexandria during the Suez crisis.

1964 Congo. The United States sent four transport planes to provide airlift for Congolese troops during a rebellion and to transport Belgian paratroopers to rescue foreigners.

1967 Congo. The United States sent three military transport aircraft with crews to provide the Congo central government with logistical support during a revolt.

1978 Zaire. From May 19 through June 1978, the United States used military transport aircraft to provide logistical support to Belgian and French rescue operations in Zaire.

1981 Libya. On August 19, 1981, U.S. planes based on the carrier U.S.S. Nimitz shot down two Libyan jets over the Gulf of Sidra after one of the Libyan jets had fired a heat-seeking missile. The United States periodically held freedom of navigation exercises in the Gulf of Sidra, claimed by Libya as territorial waters but considered international waters by the United States.

1983 Egypt. After a Libyan plane bombed a city in Sudan on March 18, 1983, and Sudan and Egypt appealed for assistance, the United States dispatched an AWACS electronic surveillance plane to Egypt.

1983 Chad. On August 8, 1983, President Reagan reported the deployment of two AWACS electronic surveillance planes and eight F-15 fighter planes and ground logistical support forces to assist Chad against Libyan and rebel forces.

1986 Libya. On March 26, 1986, President Reagan reported to Congress that, on March 24 and 25, U.S. forces, while engaged in freedom of navigation exercises around the Gulf of Sidra, had been attacked by Libyan missiles and the United States had responded with missiles.

1986 Libya. On April 16, 1986, President Reagan reported that U.S. air and naval forces had conducted bombing strikes on terrorist facilities and military installations in Libya.

1989 Libya. On January 4, 1989, two U.S. Navy F-14 aircraft based on the U.S.S. John F. Kennedy shot down two Libyan jet fighters over the Mediterranean Sea about 70 miles north of Libya. The U.S. pilots said the Libyan planes had demonstrated hostile intentions.

1990 Liberia. On August 6, 1990, President Bush reported that a reinforced rifle company had been sent to provide additional security to the U.S. Embassy in Monrovia, and that helicopter teams had evacuated U.S. citizens from Liberia.

1991 Zaire. On September 25-27, 1991, after widespread looting and rioting broke out in Kinshasa, U.S. Air Force C-141s transported 100 Belgian troops and equipment into Kinshasa. U.S. planes also carried 300 French troops into the Central African Republic and hauled back American citizens and third country nationals from locations outside Zaire.

1992 Sierra Leone. On May 3, 1992, U.S. military planes evacuated Americans from Sierra Leone, where military leaders had overthrown the government.

1992 Somalia. On December 10, 1992, President Bush reported that he had deployed U.S. armed forces to Somalia in response to a humanitarian crisis and a U.N. Security Council Resolution determining that the situation constituted a threat to international peace. This operation, called Operation Restore Hope, was part of a U.S.-led United Nations Unified Task Force (UNITAF) and came to an end on May 4, 1993. U.S. forces continued to participate in the successor United Nations Operation in Somalia (UNOSOM II), which the U.N. Security Council authorized to assist Somalia in political reconciliation and restoration of peace.

1993 Somalia. On June 10, 1993, President Clinton reported that in response to attacks against U.N. forces in Somalia by a factional leader, the U.S. Quick Reaction Force in the area had participated in military action to quell the violence. On July 1 President Clinton reported further air and ground military operations on June 12 and June 17 aimed at neutralizing military capabilities that had impeded U.N. efforts to deliver humanitarian relief and promote national reconstruction, and additional instances occurred in the following months.

1994 Rwanda. On April 12, 1994, President Clinton reported that combat-equipped U.S. military forces had been deployed to Burundi to conduct possible non-combatant evacuation operations of U.S. citizens and other third-country nationals from Rwanda, where widespread fighting had broken out. By September 30, 1994, all U.S. troops had departed from Rwanda and surrounding nations. In the Defense Appropriations Act for FY1995 (P.L. 103-335, signed September 30, 1994), Congress barred use of funds for U.S. military participation in or around Rwanda after October 7, 1994, except for any action necessary to protect U.S. citizens.

1995 Somalia. On March 1, 1995, President Clinton reported that on February 27, 1995, 1,800 combat-equipped U.S. armed forces personnel began deployment into Mogadishu, Somalia, to assist in the withdrawal of U.N. forces assigned there to the United Nations Operation in Somalia (UNOSOM II). This mission was completed on March 3, 1995.

1996 Liberia. On April 11, 1996, President Clinton reported to Congress that on April 9, 1996 due to the "deterioration of the security situation and the resulting threat to American citizens" in Liberia he had ordered U.S. military forces to evacuate from that country "private U.S. citizens and certain third-country nationals who had taken refuge in the U.S. Embassy compound.... "

1996 Liberia. On May 20, 1996, President Clinton reported to Congress the continued deployment of U.S. military forces in Liberia to evacuate both American citizens and other foreign personnel, and to respond to various isolated "attacks on the American Embassy complex" in Liberia. The President noted that the deployment of U.S. forces would continue until there was no longer any need for enhanced security at the Embassy and a requirement to maintain an evacuation capability in the country.

Appendix B. (Continued)

1996 Central African Republic. On May 23, 1996, President Clinton reported to Congress the deployment of U.S. military personnel to Bangui, Central African Republic, to conduct the evacuation from that country of "private U.S. citizens and certain U.S. Government employees," and to provide "enhanced security for the American Embassy in Bangui."

1996 Rwanda and Zaire. On December 2, 1996, President Clinton reported to Congress that to support the humanitarian efforts of the United Nations regarding refugees in Rwanda and the Great Lakes Region of Eastern Zaire, he had authorized the use of U.S. personnel and aircraft, including AC-130U planes to help in surveying the region in support of humanitarian operations, although fighting still was occurring in the area, and U.S. aircraft had been subject to fire when on flight duty.

1997 Congo and Gabon. On March 27, 1997, President Clinton reported to Congress that, on March 25, 1997, a standby evacuation force of U.S. military personnel had been deployed to Congo and Gabon to provide enhanced security for American private citizens, government employees, and selected third country nationals in Zaire, and to be available for any necessary evacuation operation.

1997 Sierra Leone. On May 30, 1997, President Clinton reported to Congress that on May 29 and May 30, 1997, U.S. military personnel were deployed to Freetown, Sierra Leone, to prepare for and undertake the evacuation of certain U.S. government employees and private U.S. citizens.

1998 Guinea-Bissau. On June 12, 1998, President Clinton reported to Congress that, on June 10, 1998, in response to an army mutiny in Guinea-Bissau endangering the U.S. Embassy, U.S. government employees and citizens in that country, he had deployed a standby evacuation force of U.S. military personnel to Dakar, Senegal, to remove such individuals, as well as selected third country nationals, from the city of Bissau. The deployment continued until the necessary evacuations were completed.

1998 Kenya and Tanzania. On August 10, 1998, President Clinton reported to Congress that he had deployed, on August 7, 1998, a Joint Task Force of U.S. military personnel to Nairobi, Kenya, to coordinate the medical and disaster assistance related to the bombings of the U.S. Embassies in Kenya and Tanzania. He also reported that teams of 50-100 security personnel had arrived in Nairobi, Kenya, and Dar es Salaam, Tanzania, to enhance the security of the U.S. Embassies and citizens there.

1998 Afghanistan and Sudan. On August 21, 1998, by letter, President Clinton reported to Congress that he had authorized airstrikes on August 20th against camps and installations in Afghanistan and Sudan used by the Osama bin Laden terrorist organization. The President did so based on what he viewed as convincing information that the bin Laden organization was responsible for the bombings, on August 7, 1998, of the U.S. Embassies in Kenya and Tanzania.

1998 Liberia. On September 29, 1998, President Clinton reported to Congress that on September 27, 1998 he had, due to political instability and civil disorder in Liberia, deployed a stand-by response and evacuation force of 30 U.S. military personnel to augment the security force at the U.S. Embassy in Monrovia, and to provide for a rapid evacuation capability, as needed, to remove U.S. citizens and government personnel from the country.

1999 Kenya. On February 25, 1999, President Clinton reported to Congress that he was continuing to deploy U.S. military personnel in that country to assist in providing security for the U.S. embassy and American citizens in Nairobi, pending completion of renovations of the American embassy facility in Nairobi, subject of a terrorist bombing in August 1998.

2000 Sierra Leone. On May 12, 2000, President Clinton, "consistent with the War Powers Resolution" reported to Congress that he had ordered a U.S. Navy patrol craft to deploy to Sierra Leone to be ready to support evacuation operations from that country if needed. He also authorized a U.S. C-17 aircraft to deliver "ammunition, and other supplies and equipment" to Sierra Leone in support of United Nations peacekeeping operations there.

2001 Terrorism threat. On September 24, 2001, President George W. Bush reported to Congress, "consistent with the War Powers Resolution," and "Senate Joint Resolution 23" that in response to terrorist attacks on the World Trade Center and the Pentagon he had ordered the "deployment of various combat-equipped and combat support forces to a number of foreign nations in the Central and Pacific Command areas of operations." The President noted in efforts to "prevent and deter terrorism" he might find it necessary to order additional forces into these and other areas of the world.... " He stated that he could not now predict "the scope and duration of these deployments," or the "actions necessary to counter the terrorist threat to the United States."

2002 Terrorism threat. On September 20, 2002, President Bush reported to Congress "consistent with the War Powers Resolution," that U.S. "combat-equipped and combat support forces" have been deployed to the Philippines since January 2002 to train with, assist and advise the Philippines' Armed Forces in enhancing their "counterterrorist capabilities." He added that U.S. forces were conducting maritime interception operations in the Central and European Command areas to combat movement, arming or financing of "international terrorists." He also noted that U.S. combat personnel had been deployed to Georgia and Yemen to help enhance the "counterterrorist capabilities" of their armed forces.

2002 Cote d'Ivoire. On September 26, 2002, President Bush reported to Congress "consistent with the War Powers Resolution," that in response to a rebellion in Cote d'Ivoire that he had on September 25, 2002 sent U.S. military personnel into Cote d'Ivoire to assist in the evacuation of American citizens and third country nationals from the city of Bouake; and otherwise assist in other evacuations as necessary.

Appendix B (Continued)

2003 Terrorism threat. On March 20, 2003, President Bush reported to Congress, "consistent with the War Powers Resolution," as well as P.L. 107-40, and "pursuant to" his authority as Commander-in-Chief, that he had continued a number of U.S. military operations globally in the war against terrorism. These military operations included ongoing U.S. actions against al-Qaeda fighters in Afghanistan; collaborative anti-terror operations with forces of Pakistan in the Pakistan/Afghanistan border area; "maritime interception operations on the high seas" in areas of responsibility of the Central and European Commands to prevent terrorist movement and other activities; and military support for the armed forces of Georgia and Yemen in counter-terrorism operations.

2003 Liberia. On June 9, 2003, President Bush reported to Congress, "consistent with the War Powers Resolution," that on June 8 he had sent about 35 combat-equipped U.S. military personnel into Monrovia, Liberia, to augment U.S. Embassy security forces, to aid in the possible evacuation of U.S. citizens if necessary. The President also noted that he had sent about 34 combat-equipped U.S. military personnel to help secure the U.S. Embassy in Nouakchott, Mauritania, and to assist in evacuation of American citizens if required. They were expected to arrive at the U.S. embassy by June 10, 2003. Back-up and support personnel were sent to Dakar, Senegal, to aid in any necessary evacuation from either Liberia or Mauritania.

2003 Liberia. On August 13, 2003, President Bush reported to Congress, "consistent with the War Powers Resolution," that in response to conditions in Liberia, on August 11, 2003, he had authorized about 4,350 U.S. combat-equipped military personnel to enter Liberian territorial waters in support of U.N. and West African States efforts to restore order and provide humanitarian assistance in Liberia.

2003 Terrorism threat. On September 19, 2003, President Bush reported to Congress "consistent with the War Powers Resolution," that U.S. "combat-equipped and combat support forces" continue to be deployed at a number of locations around the world as part of U.S. anti-terrorism efforts. American forces support anti-terrorism efforts in the Philippines, and maritime interception operations continue on the high seas in the Central, European, and Pacific Command areas of responsibility, to "prevent the movement, arming, or financing of international terrorists." He also noted that "U.S. combat equipped and support forces" had been deployed to Georgia and Djibouti to help in enhancing their "counterterrorist capabilities."

2004 Terrorism/Bosnia and Haiti. On March 20, 2004, the President reported to Congress "consistent with the War Powers Resolution," a consolidated report giving details of multiple on-going United States military deployments and operations "in support of the global war on terrorism (including in Afghanistan)," as well as operations in Bosnia and Herzegovina, Kosovo, and Haiti. In this report, the President noted that U.S. anti-terror related activities were underway in Georgia, Djibouti, Kenya, Ethiopia, Yemen, and Eritrea. He further noted that U.S. combat-equipped military personnel continued to be deployed in Kosovo as part of the NATO-led KFOR (1,900 personnel); in Bosnia and Herzegovina as part of the NATO-led SFOR (about 1,100 personnel); and approximately 1,800 military personnel were deployed in Haiti as part of the U.N. Multinational Interim Force.

2004 Terrorism threat/Horn of Africa/Kosovo/Bosnia/Iraq. On November 4, 2004, the President sent to Congress, "consistent with the War Powers Resolution," a consolidated report giving details of multiple ongoing United States military deployments and operations "in support of the global war on terrorism." These deployments, support or military operations include activities in Afghanistan, Djibouti, as well as Kenya, Ethiopia, Eritrea, Bosnia and Herzegovina, and Kosovo. In this report, the President noted that U.S. anti-terror related activities were underway in Djibouti, Kenya, Ethiopia, Yemen, and Eritrea. He further noted that U.S. combat-equipped military personnel continued to be deployed in Kosovo as part of the NATO-led KFOR (1,800 personnel); and in Bosnia and Herzegovina as part of the NATO-led SFOR (about 1,000 personnel). Meanwhile, he stated that the United States continues to deploy more than 135,000 military personnel in Iraq.

2005 Terrorism threat/Horn of Africa/Kosovo/Bosnia. On May 20, 2005, the President sent to Congress "consistent with the War Powers Resolution," a consolidated report giving details of multiple ongoing United States military deployments and operations "in support of the global war on terrorism," as well as operations in Iraq, where about 139,000 U.S. military personnel were deployed. U.S. forces are also deployed in Kenya, Ethiopia, Yemen, Eritrea, and Djibouti assisting in "enhancing counter-terrorism capabilities" of these nations. The President further noted that U.S. combat-equipped military personnel continued to be deployed in Kosovo as part of the NATO-led KFOR (1,700 personnel). Approximately 235 U.S. personnel are also deployed in Bosnia and Herzegovina as part of the NATO Headquarters-Sarajevo who assist in defense reform and perform operational tasks, such as counter terrorism and supporting the International Criminal Court for the Former Yugoslavia.

2005 Terrorism threat/Horn of Africa/Kosovo/Bosnia/Iraq. On December 7, 2005, the President sent to Congress "consistent with the War Powers Resolution," a consolidated report giving details of multiple ongoing United States military deployments and operations "in support of the global war on terrorism," and in support of the Multinational Force in Iraq, where about 160,000 U.S. military personnel were deployed. U.S. forces were also deployed in the Horn of Africa region—Kenya, Ethiopia, Yemen, and Djibouti—assisting in "enhancing counter-terrorism capabilities" of these nations. The President further noted that U.S. combat-equipped military personnel continued to be deployed in Kosovo as part of the NATO-led KFOR (1,700 personnel). Approximately 220 U.S. personnel were also deployed in Bosnia and Herzegovina as part of the NATO Headquarters-Sarajevo who assist in defense reform and perform operational tasks, such as "counter-terrorism and supporting the International Criminal Court for the Former Yugoslavia."

Appendix B (Continued)

2006 Terrorism threat/Kosovo/Bosnia/Iraq. On June 15, 2006, the President sent to Congress "consistent with the War Powers Resolution," a consolidated report giving details of multiple ongoing United States military deployments and operations "in support of the war on terror," and in Kosovo, Bosnia and Herzegovina, and as part of the Multinational Force (M.F.) in Iraq. About 131,000 military personnel were deployed in Iraq. U.S. forces were also deployed in the Horn of Africa region, and in Djibouti to support necessary operations against al-Qaida and other international terrorists operating in the region. U.S. military personnel continue to support the NATO-led Kosovo Force (KFOR). The U.S. contribution to KFOR was about 1,700 military." personnel. The NATO Headquarters-Sarajevo was established in November 22, 2004 as a successor to its stabilization operations in Bosnia-Herzegovina to continue to assist in implementing the peace agreement. Approximately 250 U.S. personnel were assigned to the NATO Headquarters-Sarajevo to assist in defense reform and perform operational tasks, such as "counter-terrorism and supporting the International Criminal Court for the Former Yugoslavia

2006 Terrorism threat/Horn of Africa/Kosovo/Bosnia. On December 15, 2006, the President sent to Congress "consistent with the War Powers Resolution," a consolidated report giving details of multiple ongoing United States military deployments and operations "in support of the war on terror," in Kosova, Bosnia and Herzegovina, and as part of the Multinational Force (M.F.) in Iraq. About 134,000 military personnel were deployed in Iraq. U.S. forces were also deployed in the Horn of Africa region, and in Djibouti to support necessary operations against al-Qaida and other international terrorists operating in the region, including Yemen. U.S. military personnel continue to support the NATO-led Kosova Force (KFOR). The U.S. contribution to KFOR was about 1,700 military personnel. The NATO Headquarters-Sarajevo was established in November 22, 2004 as a successor to its stabilization operations in Bosnia-Herzegovina to continue to assist in implementing the peace agreement. Approximately 100 U.S. personnel were assigned to the NATO Headquarters-Sarajevo to assist in defense reform and perform operational tasks, such as "counter-terrorism and supporting the International Criminal Court for the Former Yugoslavia."

2007 Terrorism threat/Kosovo/Afghanistan. On June 15 and December 14, 2007, the President sent to Congress "consistent with the War Powers Resolution," a consolidated report giving details of ongoing United States military deployments and operations "in support of the war on terror,"and in support of the NATO-led Kosovo Force (KFOR). The President reported that various U.S. "combat-equipped and combat-support forces" were deployed to "a number of locations in the Central, Pacific, European, and Southern Command areas of operation" and were engaged in combat operations against al-Qaida terrorists and their supporters.

2008 Terrorism threat/Kosovo/Afghanistan. On June 13 and December 16, 2008, the President sent to Congress "consistent with the War Powers Resolution," a consolidated report giving details of ongoing United States military deployments and operations "in support of the war on terror,"and in support of the NATO-led Kosovo Force (KFOR). The President reported that various U.S. "combat-equipped and combat-support forces" were deployed to "a number of locations in the Central, Pacific, European, Southern and Africa Command areas of operation" and were engaged in combat operations against al-Qaida terrorists and their supporters.

Source: CRS Report RL32170, Instances of Use of United States Armed Forces Abroad, 1798-2008, by Richard F. Grimmett.

Appendix C. Acronyms

ACBSP	African Coastal and Border Security Program
ACOTA	African Contingency Operations Training and Assistance
ACSS	Africa Center for Strategic Studies
AFRICOM	Africa Command
AMIS	African Union Mission in Sudan
AMISOM	African Union Mission in Somalia
AMSD	Air & Maritime Sector Development
AOR	Area of Responsibility
AU	African Union
CENTCOM	Central Command
CJTF-HOA	Combined Joint Task Force - Horn of Africa
CTFP	Regional Defense Counter-Terrorism Fellowship Program
COCOM	Combatant Command
DOD	Department of Defense
DOS	Department of State
ECOWAS	Economic Community of West African States
EDA	Excess Defense Articles
EUCOM	European Command
FMF	Foreign Military Financing
FMS	Foreign Military Sales
FOC	Full Operating Capability
GPOI	Global Peace Operations Initiative
GWOT	Global War on Terrorism

IMET	International Military Education and Training
IO	Information Operations
IOC	Initial Operating Capability
JCS	Joint Chiefs of Staff
JFCOM	Joint Forces Command
JIACG	Joint Interagency Coordination Groups
LANTCOM	Atlantic Command
MIO	Maritime Interception Operation
NATO	North Atlantic Treaty Organization
NEO	Non-Combatant Evacuation and Repatriation Operations
NORTHCOM	Northern Command
OEF-TS	Operation Enduring Freedom—Trans Sahara
OMA	USAID Office of Military Affairs
OOV	Operation Objective Voice
OSC	Office of Security Cooperation
OSD	Office of the Secretary of Defense
PACOM	Pacific Command
POLAD	Foreign Policy Advisor
REDCOM	Readiness Command
SADC	Southern African Development Community
SDA	Senior Development Advisor
SJFHQ	Standing Joint Force Headquarters
SOCOM	Special Operations Command
SOUTHCOM	Southern Command
STRATCOM	Strategic Command
STRICOM	Strike Command
TRANSCOM	Transportation Command
TSC	Theater Security Cooperation
TSCTP	Trans-Sahara Counter-Terrorism Partnership
UCP	Unified Command Plan
UNITAF	U.S. United Task Force
UNOSOM	U.N. Operation in Somalia
USAID	United States Agency for International Development

REFERENCES

[1] The White House Office of the Press Secretary, "President Bush Creates a Department of Defense Unified Combatant Command for Africa," February 6, 2007. Secretary of Defense Robert Gates announced the command's creation to Congress in testimony before the Senate Armed Services Committee on the same day. Formal efforts to establish an Africa Command, or AFRICOM, began in mid-2006, under former U.S. Secretary of Defense Donald Rumsfeld. DOD announced that it was considering AFRICOM in August 2006, and President Bush reportedly approved the proposal on December 15, 2006. "Africa Command Plans Approved by Bush, DOD Officials Confirm," *Stars and Stripes*, December 30, 2006.

[2] A unified combatant command is defined as "a command with a broad continuing mission under a single commander and composed of significant assigned components of two or more Military Departments that is established and so designated by the President, through the Secretary of Defense with the advice and assistance of the Chairman of the Joint Chiefs of Staff," according to DOD's Dictionary of Military and Associated Terms.

[3] When first announced, the draft mission statement was: "U.S. Africa Command promotes U.S. National Security objectives by working with African states and regional organizations to help strengthen stability and security in the AOR. U.S. Africa Command leads the in-theater DOD response to support other USG agencies in implementing USG security policies and strategies. In concert with other U.S. government agencies and other international partners, U.S. Africa Command conducts theater security cooperation activities to assist in building security capacity and improve accountable governance. As directed, U.S. Africa Command conducts military operations to deter aggression and respond to crises." Its current mission statement, approved by General Ward and Secretary Gates, is "United States Africa Command, in concert with other U.S. government agencies and international partners, conducts sustained security engagement through military-to-military programs, military sponsored activities, and other military operations as directed to promote a stable and secure African environment in support of U.S. foreign policy."

[4] Testimony before the Senate Armed Services Committee, September 19, 2006.

[5] Greg Mills, "World's Biggest Military Comes to Town," *Business Day*, February 9, 2007.
[6] Western Sahara is considered an "Area of Interest."
[7] For more information see http://www.defenselink.mil/specials/unified command.
[8] "Pentagon: AFRICOM Won't Boost U.S. Troop Presence on the Continent," *Inside the Army*, February 12, 2007.
[9] DOD defines stability operations as "military and civilian activities conducted across the spectrum from peace to conflict to establish or maintain order in States and regions."
[10] DOD, Directive 3000.05: Military Support for Stability, Security, Transition, and Reconstruction (SSTR) Operations, November 28, 2005. The directive also clarifies that DOD sees its role in U.S. government plans for SSTR as a supporting one: "Many stability operations tasks are best performed by indigenous, foreign, or U.S. civilian professionals. Nonetheless, U.S. military forces shall be prepared to perform all tasks necessary to establish or maintain order when civilians cannot do so."
[11] Some analysts view four traditional phases for a military campaign: deter/engage, seize initiative, decisive operations, and transition. DOD officials have begun using a phrase, "Phase Zero" to encompass efforts prior to the first phase aimed at preventing the conflict. For more information on the Phase Zero strategy and TSC, also known as peacetime engagement, see General Charles Wald, "The Phase Zero Campaign," *Joint Force Quarterly*, Issue 43, 4th Quarter 2006, available at http://www.ndu.edu/inss.
[12] DOD, FY20 10 Budget Request, available at http://www.defenselink.mil/comptroller/budget.html.
[13] Advance Questions for General Bantz J. Craddock, USA, Nominee for United States European Command and Supreme Allied Commander, Europe, in his confirmation hearing before the Senate Armed Services Committee on September 19, 2006.
[14] Interviews by author with AFRICOM officials in Germany in February 2009.
[15] While the Phase Zero approach to ensuring national security has been accepted by much of the DOD leadership, discussion is ongoing within the Department about how best to use the U.S. military in a conflict role.

[16] J. Peter Pham, "Getting AFRICOM Right," *World Defense Review*, February 15, 2007.
[17] DOD, "News Briefing with Principal Deputy Under Secretary Henry From the Pentagon," February 7, 2007.
[18] 18 See, for example, Lisa Schirch and Aaron Kishbaugh, "Leveraging '3D' Security: From Rhetoric to Reality," Foreign Policy in Focus, Policy Brief Vol. 11, No. 2, November 15, 2006.
[19] Comments by then-Principal Deputy Under Secretary of Defense Ryan Henry at a Meeting of USAID's Advisory Committee on Voluntary Foreign Aid (ACVFA) on May 23, 2007.
[20] For more information on Foreign Policy Advisors (formerly known as Political Advisors), see http://www.state.gov/ t/pm/polad/.
[21] For more information on JIACGs, see JFCOM's fact sheet at http://www.jfcom.mil/about/facts_prt/JIACG.pdf and Col. Matthew F. Bogdanos, "Joint Interagency Cooperation: The First Step," *Joint Forces Quarterly*, Issue 37, 2005.
[22] These offices are also sometimes referred to as Offices of Defense Cooperation (ODC) or Security Assistance Organizations (SAOs). There are currently 15 OSCs in Africa (not including Egypt) and over 30 defense attaches in U.S. embassies on the continent. AFRICOM plans to open new OSCs in Cameroon, Chad, Libya, and Rwanda in FY20 10, contingent on approval in the FY20 10 Foreign Operations Appropriation. Changes to the titles and responsibilities of defense attaches and security assistance officers were made in DOD Directive 5105.75 in December 2007.
[23] A theater campaign plan translates national or theater strategy into operational concepts.
[24] As in the case of POLADs, DOD and the respective department or agency will establish an agreement regarding the relationship between the staff member and the command.
[25] DOD, "News Briefing with Principal Deputy Under Secretary Henry From the Pentagon," April 27, 2007.
[26] U.S. military facilities on the island of Diego Garcia, in the Indian Ocean, will remain under the AOR of PACOM.
[27] DOD, "News Briefing with Principal Deputy Under Secretary Henry From the Pentagon," April 23, 2007.
[28] The mission transfer process from CENTCOM to AFRICOM for CJTF-HOA responsibilities continued into 2009.

[29] DOD has spent approximately $140 million between FY2007 and FY2009 to renovate the Stuttgart facilities.

[30] Comments by then-Principal Deputy Under Secretary of Defense Ryan Henry at a Public Meeting of USAID's Advisory Committee on Voluntary Foreign Aid (ACVFA) on May 23, 2007.

[31] DOD's FY2009 Budget Request Summary Justification can be found at http://www.defenselink.mil/comptroller/ budget.html

[32] For more information on Article 98 agreements, see CRS Report RL31495, *U.S. Policy Regarding the International Criminal Court* (ICC), by Jennifer K. Elsea.

[33] Testimony before the Defense Subcommittee of the House Appropriations Committee at a hearing on the U.S. Africa Command, March 19, 2009.

[34] These figures do not necessarily include contractors working at command headquarters.

[35] AFRICOM had 628 military positions, 318 DOD civilian positions, and 13 interagency positions (not including liaison positions) assigned as of October 1, 2008. These figures were short of the approved FY2009 targets: 639 military positions, 665 DOD civilian positions, and 52 interagency positions. For more information, see Government Accountability Office, *Force Structure: Preliminary Observations on the Progress and Challenges Associated with Establishing the U.S. Africa Command*, GAO-08-947T, July 15, 2008.

[36] AFRICOM's four service component commands are: U.S. Army Africa/Southern European Task Force (ARAF/SETAF); U.S. Naval Forces, Africa (NAVAF); U.S. Marine Forces, Africa (MARFORAF); and U.S. Air Forces Africa/ the 17th Air Force (AFAFRICA). Its joint theater special operations command is called Special Operations Command, Africa (SOCAF). They are located, respectively, in Vicenza, Italy; Naples, Italy; Stuttgart, Germany; Ramstein, Germany; and Stuttgart, Germany.

[37] These estimates were provided to the author by AFRICOM officials in October 2008.

[38] For more information, see CRS Report RL34473, *Defense: FY2009 Authorization and Appropriations*, by Pat Towell, Stephen Daggett, and Amy Belasco.

[39] In interviews with the author in December 2008, DOD officials reported that a compromise had been reached on the cut to salaries for interagency personnel.

[40] The $278 request is divided into the following: $74 million for civilian pay; $87 million for COCOM mission support; $47 million for Operation Enduring Freedom – Trans-Sahara; $38 million for Theater Security Cooperation/OSCs; $25 million for the SJFHQ; and $8 million for Operation Objective Voice. For more information on the FY20 10 DOD budget, see CRS Report R40567, *Defense: FY2010 Authorization and Appropriations*, coordinated by Pat Towell.

[41] Camp Lemonier received $68.6 million in military construction projects in FY2008 and approximately $31.4 million in FY2009.

[42] Requested funding for CJTF-HOA operations in FY20 10 is $60 million; requested funding for base operating costs and facilities modification at Lemonier is $249 million.

[43] For an overview of the history of U.S. military involvement in Africa, see Appendix A. Appendix B provides a list of instances in which U.S. military forces have deployed in conflict situations in Africa since World War II.

[44] Letitia Lawson, "U.S. Africa Policy Since the Cold War," *Strategic Insights*, Vol. VI, Issue 1, January 2007.

[45] The report did, however, note significant U.S. political and humanitarian interests. DOD Office of International Security Affairs, United States Security Strategy for Sub-Saharan Africa, August 1995.

[46] The White House, *The National Security Strategy of the United States*, September 2002.

[47] The White House, *The National Security Strategy of the United States*, March 2006.

[48] Some U.S. officials have recently argued that environmental security should be added as a national security issue, particularly as it relates to Africa. One DOD official testified before Congress that climate change served as a "threat multiplier" in Africa, using Nigeria, Sudan, and Somalia as examples and asserting, "beyond the more conventional threats we traditionally address, I believe we must now also prepare to respond to the consequences of dramatic population migrations, pandemic health issues and significant food and water shortages due to the possibility of significant climate change." Testimony of General Charles Wald, Member, Military Advisory Board, at a hearing on Climate Change and National Security Threats by the Senate Foreign Relations Committee on May 9, 2007.

[49] Walter H. Kansteiner III and J. Stephen Morrison, *Rising U.S. Stakes in Africa: Seven Proposals to Strengthen U.S.- Africa Policy*, CSIS, May 2004.

[50] See John Authers, "The Short View: African Oil," Financial Times, April 24, 2007. Data on U.S. crude oil imports is compiled by the Department of Energy's Energy Information Administration, and is available at http://www.eia.doe.gov

[51] The White House, "President Delivers State of the Union Address," January 31, 2006.

[52] The White House, *The National Security Strategy of the United States*, September 2002.

[53] Greg Jaffe, "In Massive Shift, U.S. Is Planning To Cut Size of Military in Germany," *Wall Street Journal*, June 10, 2003.

[54] Central Intelligence Agency, *Global Trends 2015: A Dialogue About the Future With Non-government Experts*, December 2000. This prediction implies that previously higher sub-Saharan African shares of U.S. oil imports will be eclipsed and then surpassed. Previously, when absolute levels of U.S. oil imports were lower, Africa provided a higher percentage of annual U.S. imports (e.g., about 19.53% in 1990 and about 18.47% in 1995) than it has during the past five years. For more information, see also African Oil Policy Initiative Group, *African Oil: A Priority for U.S. National Security and African Development*, January 2002.

[55] According to the International Maritime Bureau, the waters off the coast of Nigeria had the highest number of attacks worldwide in 2007, but attacks by Somali pirates were the most numerous in 2008.

[56] The White House, *The National Strategy for Maritime Security*, September 20, 2005.

[57] "U.S. Increasing Operations in Gulf of Guinea," American Forces Press Service, September 5, 2006.

[58] For more information see CRS Report R40528, *Piracy off the Horn of Africa*, by Lauren Ploch et al..

[59] For further discussion on the indirect costs of instability, see CRS Report 97-454, *Peacekeeping Options: Considerations for U.S. Policymakers and the Congress*, by Marjorie Ann Browne, Ellen Collier, and Nina M. Serafino.

[60] Current operations in Africa include UNAMID (Darfur region of Sudan), UNMIS (Sudan), UNOCI (Cote d'Ivoire), UNMIL (Liberia),

MONUC (Dem. Rep. Of Congo), MINURCAT (Chad/CAR), and MINURSO (Western Sahara).

[61] For more information see CRS Report RL32773, *The Global Peace Operations Initiative: Background and Issues for Congress*, by Nina M. Serafino.

[62] The White House, *The National Security Strategy of the United States*, September 2002.

[63] Hearing Transcript of the Senate Armed Services Committee, "Current and Future Worldwide Threats to the National Security of the United States," March 10, 2009.

[64] See, for example, the testimony of General Ward at a Senate Armed Services Committee hearing on AFRICOM, March 17, 2009.

[65] Speech by DOD official Vincent Kern referenced in "Africa Is Still Ripe for Terrorism, Top Pentagon Official Asserts," *The Washington File*, February 10, 2004.

[66] Jessica Piombo, "Terrorism and U.S. Counter-Terrorism Programs in Africa: An Overview," *Strategic Insights*, Vol. VI, Issue 1, January 2007.

[67] The White House, *The National Security Strategy of The United States*, September 2002.

[68] See Douglas Farah, "Al Qaeda Cash Tied to Diamond Trade Sale of Gems From Sierra Leone Rebels Raised Millions, Sources Say," *The Washington Post*, November 2, 2001; U.N. Security Council, Report of the Panel of Experts Pursuant to Security Council Resolution 1343 (2001), Paragraph 19, Concerning Liberia, in S/2001/1015, October 26, 2001; and CRS Report RL3 075 1, *Diamonds and Conflict: Background, Policy, and Legislation*, by Nicolas Cook.

[69] Stephen D. Krasner and Carlos Pascual, "Addressing State Failure," *Foreign Affairs*, Vol. 84, No. 4, July/August 2005.

[70] UNAIDS, 2008 Report on the Global AIDS Epidemic, July 2008.

[71] Speech by Secretary Powell at the Gheskio Clinic, Port-au-Prince, Haiti, April 5, 2004.

[72] Kevin A. O'Brien, "Headlines Over the Horizon: AIDS and African Armies," *Atlantic Monthly*, Vol. 292, No. 1, July/August 2003.

[73] For more information, see CRS Report RL33584, *AIDS in Africa*, by Nicolas Cook.

[74] General Ward, in his confirmation hearing, has testified that "The U.S. military is not an instrument of first resort in providing humanitarian assistance but supports civilian relief agencies ... The U.S. military may

be involved when it provides a unique service; when the civilian response is overwhelmed; and civilian authorities request assistance. The USAID Office of Disaster Assistance validates all such requests for U.S. military assistance. Our role in this context will not change."

[75] DOD defines a "contingency operation" as a military operation in which members of the Armed Forces are or may become involved, either by designation of the Secretary of Defense or by law, in military actions, operations, or hostilities against an enemy of the United States or against an opposing force.

[76] For more information on U.S. Foreign Military Training programs, see the Department of State's website at http://www.state.gov/t/pm/rls/rpt/fmtrpt.

[77] U.S. State Department, "Africa Center for Strategic Studies Opens Annex in Ethiopia," August 1, 2006, available at http://usinfo.state.gov.

[78] For more information, see http://www.dsca.osd.mil/ or CRS Report RL33758, *U.S. Arms Sales: Agreements with and Deliveries to Major Clients, 1998-2005*, by Richard F. Grimmett.

[79] The website can be found at http://www.magharebia.com.

[80] For more information, see http://www.hoa.centcom.mil/resources/english/facts.asp.

[81] U.S. Central Command, "CJTF HOA donates supplies to Djiboutian Well Drillers," March 12, 2007.

[82] For more information, see http://www.hoa.centcom.mil/resources/english/facts.asp.

[83] For more information on CJTF-HOA activities, see http://www.hoa.centcom.mil.

[84] DOD, "News Briefing with Principal Deputy Under Secretary Henry From the Pentagon," April 23, 2007.

[85] As of 2009, SPP included seven U.S-African partnerships: Utah and Morocco, North Dakota and Ghana, California and Nigeria, Wyoming and Tunisia, New York and California, North Carolina and Botswana, and Vermont and Senegal.

[86] The ASF is divided into North, West, Central, East, and South Regional Brigades, which are organized by the Community of Sahel-Saharan States (CENSAD), the Economic Community of West African States (ECOWAS), the Economic Community of Central African States (ECCAS/CEMAC), the states within the Inter-Governmental Authority on Development (IGAD), and the Southern African Development Community (SADC), respectively.

[87] Other authorities used for DOD training include the Combatant Commander Initiative Fund (Title 10, USC, Sec. 166(a)), the DOD Regional Counter-Terrorism Fellowship Program (Title 10, USC, Sec. 2249(c)), the Air Force's Aviation Leadership Program (Title 10, USC, Sec. 9381-9383), training with U.S. Special Forces (Title 10, USC, Sec. 2011), and disaster response training under Title 10, USC, Sec. 2561.

[88] For more information on Global Fleet Stations, see U.S. Department of the Navy, Naval Operations Concept 2006, Washington, 2006. See also "U.S. Navy Seeks to Expand Presence in W. Africa," DefenseNews, June 4, 2007;"U.S. Naval Forces Europe Prepares For AFRICOM Stand Up," American Forces Press Service, June 1, 2007; and "U.S. Navy Plans Six-Month West African Training Mission," USINFO, June 7, 2007.

[89] Presentation by Admiral Harry Ulrich, Commander, U.S. Naval Forces Europe, at the Center for Strategic and International Studies on October 16, 2007.

[90] House Rpt. 111-230, accompanying H.R. 3326, the Department of Defense Appropriations Bill, 2010, expresses support for more robust deployment of APS and recommends an additional $20.5 million in support of maritime security capacity building in AFRICOM's AOR.

[91] U.S. State Department, "Africa Overview," *Country Reports on Terrorism,* April 30, 2007.

[92] Libya was recently invited to join TSCTP.

[93] U.S. Department of State, *FY 2008 Performance Summary*, February 2008.

[94] For more information, see CRS Report RL32773, *The Global Peace Operations Initiative: Background and Issues for Congress*, by Nina M. Serafino.

[95] For U.S. reactions, see, for example, Michael Moran, "The New 'Africa Command,'" Council on Foreign Relations, February 9, 2007; Brett D. Schaefer, "Creating an Africa Command: Bush Administration Makes the Right Call," Heritage Foundation, February 7, 2007; "Analysts Concerned New US Military Command to Hamper African Development," VOA, October 23, 2007; Mark Malan, U.S. Civil-Military Imbalance for Global Engagement: Lessons From the Operational Level in Africa, Refugees International, July 2008; and Daniel Volman and William Minter, "AFRICOM – Making Peace or Fueling War," *Foreign Policy in Focus,* March 13, 2009.

[96] See, for example, "The U.S., Oil, and Africa," *Egyptian Mail*, February 20, 2007.

[97] Dulue Mbachu, "Skepticism Over U.S. Africa Command," *ISN Security Watch*, February 19, 2007.

[98] See, for example, "Morocco Lobbying to Become Home for New U.S. Military Command," *Middle East Newsline*, February 9, 2007, and "Algerian Foreign Minister "Satisfied" With Plans for US-Africa Command," *El-Khabar*, March 24, 2007.

[99] DOD, "News Briefing with Principal Deputy Under Secretary Henry from the Pentagon," April 23, 2007.

[100] DOD, "DOD Special Briefing on Africa Command with Mr. Ryan Henry from the Pentagon," June 21, 2007.

[101] "U.S. Army Boss for Africa Says No Garrisons Planned," Reuters, November 8, 2007.

[102] Some details of the debate are included in "Gaborone Succeeds At PAP As Sebetela is Booed," All Africa, October 29, 2007.

[103] "West African Military Heads Want to Hear More from the United States on Africa Command," Associated Press, November 7, 2007.

[104] White House Press Release, "President Bush Meets with President Umaru Yar'Adua of the Federal Republic of Nigeria," December 13, 2007.

[105] "AFRICOM Ship Heads for the Gulf of Guinea," *This Day* (Lagos), January 8, 2008.

[106] Press availability with Presidents Bush and Kufour in Accra, Ghana on February 20, 2008, available at http://www.whitehouse.gov

[107] Authorities provided to DOD under Title 10, USC, cannot be generally used for training or equipment programs, whereas Title 22 funds, which are controlled by the State Department, but which include some DOD-implemented programs like FMF and IMET, cannot be used to fund military operations. In the FY2006 Defense Authorization Act (P.L. 109-163), Congress gave DOD expanded funding and authorities under Title 10, USC, Section 1206 and 1207 to address lengthy administrative and procurement delays. Section 1206 authorities allow DOD to directly fund some security cooperation activities. In FY2006, DOD obligated $13 million in Section 1206 funding to African countries. In FY2007, over $47 million was obligated for African recipients, and in FY2008 approximately $62 million was obligated. In July 2009, DOD submitted to Congress its first tranche of FY2009 1206 programs, including $46.4 million for Africa. At the request of Senator Richard Lugar, the GAO

compiled a report, Section 1206 Security Assistance Program—Findings on Criteria, Coordination, and Implementation, in February 2007.

[108] In his testimony before the Senate Armed Services Committee on May 17, 2007,the EUCOM Commander expressed concern that Article 98 restrictions could affect long-term U.S.-African security relationships and hinder the logistical capability of countries that do not sign Article 98 agreements to participate in regional peacekeeping efforts.

[109] Congress has, in the past, prohibited funding for combatant commands. For example, under the FY1982 DOD Authorization Act (P.L. 97-252), Congress prohibited the use of funds for the integration of the Army's Military Traffic Management Command and the Navy's Military Sealift Command into a new unified transportation command, at the request of the Army and Navy Chiefs of Staff.

[110] Then-EUCOM Commander Bantz Craddock told a Defense Writers Group forum on May 18, 2007, "It will be difficult to get subscription and participation by the interagency." Other concerns have been expressed to the author in interviews with Administration officials.

[111] See, for example, the speech delivered by Secretary Gates to the U.S. Global Leadership Campaign in Washington, DC, on July 15, 2008.

[112] Some of the challenges in coordinating a more effective interagency process were outlined by John Hamre, President of the Center for Strategic and International Studies (CSIS), in a hearing, "Organizing Department of Defense Roles and Mission Requirements," held by the House Armed Services Committee on June 20, 2007.

[113] Statement of Senator Russ Feingold, "Creation of a U.S. Africa Command," before the Senate on January 10, 2007.

[114] Senate Foreign Affairs Committee, Embassies as Command Posts in the Anti-Terror Campaign, December 15, 2006.

[115] Statements of Senator Russ Feingold, "Creation of a U.S. Africa Command," before the Senate on January 10, 2007, and on January 27, 2009.

[116] Opening Statement at the Senate Foreign Relations Committee hearing "Exploring The U.S. Africa Command and A New Strategic Relationship With Africa," August 1, 2007.

[117] Other former U.S. military installations in North Africa included Kenitra Naval Air Station, also known as Port Lyautey, and several Naval Communication Relay Stations in Morocco, as well as three airbases: Nouassur, Sidi Slimane, and Ben Guerir.

[118] The White House, "Statement by Principal Deputy Press Secretary Speaks on the United States Air Strike Against Libya," April 15, 1986.

[119] See the speech of President George H.W. Bush before a Joint Session of Congress, "*Toward a New World Order*," September 11, 1990.

[120] See the statement of then-U.S. Ambassador to the United Nations Madeline Albright before the House Foreign Affairs Committee, "Myths of Peacekeeping," June 24, 1993.

[121] For more information, see CRS Report RL30065, *Somalia: Background and U.S. Involvement Through the 1990s*, by Ted Dagneand CRS Report RL30184, *Military Interventions by U.S. Forces from Vietnam to Bosnia: Background, Outcomes, and "Lessons Learned" for Kosovo*, by Nina M. Serafino.

[122] Twenty-nine American soldiers ultimately lost their lives as a result of the conflict in Somalia.

[123] Although the mission was deemed successful in alleviating the starvation and disease that threatened the refugees, many have been highly critical of the United States, the United Nations, and others for not doing more to attempt to avert the genocide that occurred in Rwanda that year. See, for example, Col. Scott R. Feil, "Could 5,000 Peacekeepers Have Saved 500,000 Rwandans?: Early Intervention Reconsidered," *ISD Reports*, Vol. III, No. 2, April 1997.

[124] DOD Office of International Security Affairs, United States Security Strategy for Sub-Saharan Africa, August 1995.

[125] According to DOD, a military operation that is either designated by the Secretary of Defense as a contingency operation or becomes a contingency operation as a matter of law: title 10, United States Code (USC), Section 101 (a)(13).

[126] For more information, see CRS Report RL32243, *Liberia: Transition to Peace*, by Nicolas Cook.

[127] John Vandiver, "AFRICOM Official Defends U.S. Role in Ugandan Mission," Stars and Stripes, February 14, 2009; Jeffrey Gettleman and Eric Schmitt, "U.S. Aided a Failed Plan to Rout Ugandan Rebels," New *York Times,* February 6, 2009.

[128] Covert actions, disaster relief, and routine alliance stationing and training exercises are not included in this list. Most instances listed since 1980 are summaries of U.S. military deployments reported to Congress by the President as a result of the War Powers Resolution.

In: U.S. Political and Trade Relations with Africa ISBN 978-1-61209-956-9
Editor: Gregory D. Ferro © 2012 Nova Science Publishers, Inc.

Chapter 3

SOUTH AFRICA: CURRENT ISSUES AND U.S. RELATIONS*

Lauren Ploch

ABSTRACT

Over a decade after the South African majority gained its independence from white minority rule under apartheid, a system of racial segregation, the Republic of South Africa is firmly established as a regional power. With Africa's largest Gross Domestic Product (GDP), a diverse economy, and a government that has played an active role in the promotion of regional peace and stability, South Africa is poised to have a substantial impact on the economic and political future of Africa. The country is twice the size of Texas and has a population of almost 50 million, of which about 80% is African and 10% white. Its political system is regarded as stable, but South Africa faces serious long-term challenges arising from poverty, unemployment, and AIDS. President Thabo Mbeki resigned in September 2008 and was replaced by interim President Kgalema Motlanthe. South Africa's most recent elections were held on April 22, 2009.

The African National Congress (ANC), which led the struggle against apartheid, has dominated the political scene since the end of apartheid and continues to enjoy widespread support in South Africa. The party fell short of retaining its two-thirds majority in the parliament

---

*This is an edited, reformatted and augmented version of CRS Report RL31697, dated May 20, 2009.

during the 2009 elections, however. Inter-party divisions, which led to Mbeki's resignation in 2008, resulted in the formation of a breakaway party, the Congress of the People (COPE). COPE received 7.4% of the 2009 vote, picking up 30 seats in the 400-seat parliament. The ANC now holds 264 seats, while the main opposition party, the Democratic Alliance (DA), holds 67 seats and gained control of one of the country's nine provinces. Jacob Zuma, elected as head of the ANC in December 2007, weathered a series of corruption charges and was chosen by the ANC-dominated parliament after the 2009 national elections to serve as South Africa's newest President. Motlanthe now serves as Deputy President.

South Africa has the largest HIV/AIDS population in the world, with almost six million South Africans reportedly HIV positive. The former Mbeki Administration's policy on HIV/AIDS was controversial. The country has weathered a series of corruption scandals, and continues to struggle with high crime and unemployment rates. Mounting social tensions related to the competition for jobs, resources, and social services led to an eruption of xenophobic violence against immigrants in mid-2008. The government and the private sector have undertaken a wide variety of construction and infrastructure projects in preparation for the upcoming 2010 soccer World Cup. South Africa has benefitted from steady economic growth in recent years, although economists predict weaker growth prospects for the near future.

South Africa is considered to be one of the United States' two strategic partners on the continent, along with Nigeria. Bilateral relations are cordial, however, the U.S. and South African administrations have expressed differences with respect to the situations in Zimbabwe, Iran, and Iraq, and U.S. officials have articulated frustration with the South African government on positions it took while serving on the United Nations Security Council. This report will be updated as events warrant.

BACKGROUND

The people of South Africa are highly diverse. Black Africans make up more than three-quarters of the population, but come from several different ethnic backgrounds. Most whites are Afrikaans speakers of Dutch, German, and French Huguenot ancestry, but there is a substantial English- speaking white minority. The remainder of the population are Asian, largely of Indian descent, and people of mixed race, widely referred to as "Coloureds."

South Africa's economy, the largest on the continent, is diverse as well. South Africa produces wine, wool, maize and other agricultural products for export, although only about 12% of the country's land is suitable for agriculture. Moreover, South Africa is the world's leading producer of gold, platinum, and chromium. Major industrial sectors include automobile assembly, chemicals, textiles, foodstuffs, and iron and steel production. South African cell phone companies and other firms are active throughout Africa, and SABMiller, formerly South African Breweries, operates on a global scale. The service sector recently surpassed mineral and energy resources as South Africa's primary income earner, according to the World Bank. The country's stock exchange is among the 20 largest in the world, and South Africa is one of the few countries on the continent to rank as an upper middle income country. Despite its many economic strengths, however, the country ranks as one of the most unequal societies in the world in terms of income distribution. The majority of black South Africans live in poverty, and South Africa's cities are surrounded by vast informal housing settlements known as "townships." Shortages of water, electricity, and other social services in the townships have contributed to growing tensions, as evidenced by a rise in township protests in recent years.

South Africa is an influential actor in the international relations of Africa. In October 2006, South Africa was elected as one of the 10 non-permanent members of the United Nations (U.N.) Security Council for a two-year term that recently expired, and it is a member of the U.N. Human Rights Council. Its voting record on both bodies has been considered by some to be controversial. South Africa was a founding member of the African Union (AU), successor to the Organization of African Unity (OAU), and then-President Thabo Mbeki served as the AU's first chairperson. President Mbeki also took a lead role in the development of the New Partnership for Africa's Development (NEPAD), an African-designed plan for improved governance within Africa and increased western aid, trade, and investment that was adopted by the AU as its economic framework. South Africa has repeatedly put itself forward as a venue for major international conferences, such as the World Summit on Sustainable Development, which met in Johannesburg in August and September 2002, and the World Conference on Racism in 2001. In 2010, South Africa will be the first African nation to host the soccer World Cup, which is expected by some to have a significant impact on the country's overall economic growth and job creation.

Civil war, weak regimes, and general instability in the region have historically had a negative impact on South Africa, and the country continues to face a large influx of illegal immigrants. By some estimates, more than three million Zimbabweans currently reside illegally in South Africa. Some South Africans blame these immigrants for the country's high crime and unemployment rates and rising food prices, and in May 2008 tensions erupted in the townships, sparking a wave of xenophobic attacks that displaced over 25,000 and left over 60 dead. The attacks could have long term consequences for attendance of the World Cup and for tourism in general.

In order to promote greater stability, former President Mbeki and South African officials have played prominent mediator roles in African conflicts, and South African troops actively support peacekeeping missions throughout the continent. In 2002, they helped to persuade the parties to the prolonged conflict in the Democratic Republic of the Congo (DRC) to sign a peace agreement following negotiations in South Africa. Mbeki was less successful in mediating the conflict in Cote d'Ivoire. Over 1,200 South African troops are currently participating as peacekeepers in the U.N. Mission in the DRC (MONUC), and the country contributed almost 900 soldiers to the U.N. Operation in Burundi (ONUB), where former President Nelson Mandela played a leading role in brokering a peace agreement.

South Africa in Brief

Population: 49 million
African, 79%; whites, 9.6%; mixed race, 9%; Asian, 2.5%
Population Growth Rate: 0.281%
Approximate size: twice the size of Texas
GDP (Official Exchange Rate): $300.4 billion
GNI per capita (Atlas Method): $5,390
Unemployment: 21.7%
Life Expectancy: 48.98 years
Prevalence of HIV/AIDS: 16.2%
Literacy: 86.4%
Religion: 80% Christian, 2% Muslim, 4% Other, 15% None
Language most often spoken at home:
Zulu, 24%; Xhosa, 18%; Afrikaans, 13%; Sepedi 9.4%,
English 8.2%, Setswana 8.2%, Sesotho 7.9%, Xitsonga 4.4%
Sources: World Bank, CIA World Factbook , UNAIDS.

South African forces also played a key role in the African Union Mission in Darfur (known by the acronym of AMIS), and now contribute to the U.N.-African Union Mission in Darfur (UNAMID) [1]. In a move believed by many to protest the Sudanese government's policies toward Darfur, the Mbeki government was instrumental in preventing Sudan from attaining the chairmanship of the African Union in 2006. It has, however, protested the imposition of tougher U.N. sanctions against Sudan as counterproductive [2]. The country has supported democratic advances elsewhere on the continent, providing millions of ballots in 2006 for elections in the DRC. In March 2007, the heads of state of the Southern African Development Community (SADC) nominated then-President Mbeki to serve as a mediator between the Zimbabwean government and the opposition in an effort to resolve that country's political and economic crises. Mbeki's role has been controversial.

POLITICAL SITUATION

The Republic of South Africa held its first universal suffrage elections in April 1994. The African National Congress (ANC), which had led the struggle against white minority rule and the apartheid system of state-enforced racial segregation, won control of the National Assembly. The Assembly chose as President Nelson Mandela, the ANC leader who had been released from prison in 1990, after serving 27 years. His release followed years of secret contacts between the ANC and key white business and political figures. These contacts had led both sides to conclude that a settlement could be negotiated that would protect the interests of all South Africans. The negotiations themselves encountered many difficulties, including several outbreaks of violence that threatened to destroy the peace process. Finally, however, in November 1993, all-party negotiations resulted in a final agreement on a new constitution and free elections, held in 1994. South Africa's second universal suffrage elections were held in June 1999, and the ANC retained control of the National Assembly. Deputy President Thabo Mbeki, who had served in key ANC posts overseas during the anti-apartheid struggle, was chosen by the Assembly to succeed Mandela. Mbeki retained his position as President following the April 2004 parliamentary elections, in which the ANC won almost 70% of the votes.

South Africa's politics continue to be dominated by the ANC, which has enjoyed support among many black South Africans because of its role in spearheading the long struggle against white minority rule. Until December 2007, when he lost the party presidency to a rival, Thabo Mbeki served as president both of the party and the country [3]. He was expected to remain President of South Africa until the 2009 elections but resigned from the position in September 2008. He was replaced by an interim president, former Deputy ANC leader Kgalema Motlanthe. Following Mbeki's resignation, several prominent members of the party led a breakaway faction, now known as the Congress of the People (COPE).

Prior to the 2009 elections, the ANC held a 72% majority of the seats in the 400-member National Assembly, where the country's legislative power principally resides, far ahead of its nearest rival, the Democratic Alliance (DA), which had 12% of the seats. The Inkatha Freedom Party (IFP), headed by Mangosuthu Buthelezi, had about 6% of Assembly seats. Buthelezi, who has been active in South African politics for decades, holds a Zulu chieftainship, and the party is largely Zulu in membership. The IFP has experienced a steady decline in parliamentary seats since the 1994 election, while the ANC and the DA have gained electoral support. Other parties represented in parliament include the New National Party (NNP, see below), the United Democratic Movement (UDM), the Independent Democrats (ID), and the African Christian Democratic Party (ACDP). The ANC also held majorities in all of South Africa's nine provincial assemblies. In addition to the National Assembly, there is a higher legislative body, the National Council of Provinces (NCOP), with limited powers. The members of NCOP are chosen by the governments of the nine provinces, all controlled by the ANC.

The Democratic Alliance

The second largest party in the National Assembly, the Democratic Alliance (DA), was created in 2000 through a merger of the Democratic Party (DP) and the New National Party (NNP), to challenge ANC dominance of the political system. The merger surprised many analysts, since the NNP was directly descended from the National Party, which had created apartheid and established the white minority regime that ruled South Africa for more than 40 years. In contrast, the DP, though also largely white, advocated a classical liberal platform and was heir to the Progressive Party, which had strongly opposed apartheid and campaigned on human rights issues.

However, by allying, the two parties were able to ensure their control of the legislature of Western Cape Province and of many local governments in the province, including the government of Cape Town, in the 2000 local elections [4].

DP leader Tony Leon, an articulate critic of the ANC with respect to the slow pace of privatization, transparency, and other issues, became DA leader, with NNP head Marthinus van Schalkwyk as his deputy. The alliance soon fragmented in a way that has further enhanced the power of the ANC in South African politics. In October 2001, van Schalkwyk announced that the NNP would leave the DA and enter into a cooperative agreement with the ANC. The NNP leader explained that the move would promote national unity and progress, while critics suggested that he was primarily interested in securing government appointments for NNP leaders [5].

Van Schalkwyk's break with the DA precipitated a prolonged national debate over "floor crossing"—that is, over whether elected NNP representatives in assemblies at the local, provincial, and national levels should be permitted to cross over from the DA to the new ANC/NNP alliance. Representatives at all levels in South Africa are elected not as individuals but because their names appear on lists selected by each party. The proportion of the vote received by a party in an election determines how many of those on its list will be given seats. Many argue that floor crossing in such a system thwarts the will of the voters, and it had not been permitted in South Africa. However, in 2002 the Constitutional Court allowed floor crossing at the local level, throwing control of Cape Town and a number of other towns to the ANC and its NNP allies. The National Assembly passed legislation in 2003 allowing MPs to change their party affiliation during two week "window periods." As a result of a September 2005 "window period," the ANC gained 14 seats, including all seven NNP parliamentarians and four DA MPs who complained of racism within the party.

Although the ANC controls the provincial government of Western Cape, the city of Cape Town remains the last major urban opposition bastion. Following a close win by the DA candidate Helen Zille in 2006, the ANC began a controversial bid to change the city's government from a mayorally-dominated system to one run by a 10-member committee, which would have left the current mayor a de facto figurehead. Subsequent criticism by the other parties appears to have persuaded the ANC to drop its proposed restructuring plan. Zille replaced Tony Leon as head of the DA party when he stepped down in May 2007 [6]. She became Premier of the Western Cape following the 2009 elections.

Strains in the ANC Alliance

The ANC has long worked in an interlocking tripartite alliance with the Congress of South African Trade Unions (COSATU) and the South African Communist Party (SACP). Leaders of COSATU and the SACP sit on the National Executive Committee (NEC) of the ANC, which is the party's principal decision-making body. However, there has been considerable disagreement among the ANC and its allies over the government's economic reform programs. The government's first major economic strategy, known as

Growth, Employment, and Redistribution (GEAR), sought to spur economic growth by attracting foreign investment, strengthening the private sector, and privatizing state-owned enterprises. COSATU and the SACP have argued that this approach has failed to benefit South Africa's poor. They favor the creation of programs that would use state resources to create jobs and a moratorium on privatization. In 2005 the general secretary of COSATU announced in a union meeting,

> We want the ANC to be maintained as an organization primarily of the workers and the poor. We will never hand over this weapon, built up with our blood, sweat, and tears, to the other side on a silver platter. We will never let the ANC be privatized by the rich. It is a working class formation and a left-wing liberation movement—it must remain ours [7].

Former President Mbeki, on the other hand, argued that the ANC was a "broad church" capable of representing socialists and nationalists and bridging class divisions.

COSATU was highly critical of Mbeki's stance on the AIDS epidemic and his approach toward the Zimbabwe situation (see below). In 2006, COSATU launched a general strike to protest the loss of 100,000 jobs over the prior three years, primarily from the textile and mining industries. In June 2007, the country's trade unions launched what was reported to have been the biggest strike since the end of apartheid, costing the economy an estimated $418 million [8]. The unions, who were demanding a 12% pay raise for public servants, accepted the government's offer of a 7.5% raise after four weeks of protest. More recent strikes, in July and August 2008, brought the country's mining industry to a standstill as workers protested rising food, fuel, and electricity costs. These strikes were considered significant acts of defiance against the policies of the Mbeki government. Speculation regarding a splintering of the ANC grew as the rift between COSATU, its populist allies, and Mbeki supporters within the ANC widened.

The Succession Debate and Mbeki's Resignation

As President Mbeki neared the end of his second term as president of the ANC, there was considerable speculation on whom the party might choose for the position at the ANC's national congress in December 2007. Mbeki had suggested that he would not run for a third term. His successor would be widely expected to succeed him as President of the country following the national elections in 2009. Although the ANC's party constitution allows for a competitive leadership race, no party presidential candidacy had ever been contested. Mbeki's dismissal of Jacob Zuma as the country's Deputy President in 2005 (see below) exposed divisions in the party (Zuma remained deputy president of the party). He had been widely considered to be the likely successor to Mbeki prior to these scandals. Zuma, a populist who has elicited strong support from both youth and labor groups, as well as from his Zulu ethnic base, has been linked with a number of controversies, including a 2006 rape allegation for which he was acquitted, and a high profile corruption case (see "The Arms Deal and Other Corruption Scandals" below). Zuma made his intention to vie for the party leadership post clear, and he was vocally supported by leaders from COSATU and SACP, who claim he has been a victim of political conspiracy. After months of speculation, Mbeki, rather than put his support behind a chosen successor, chose to run for a third term as ANC president. Zuma won a decisive victory over Mbeki in a secret ballot vote at the party congress, suggesting that Mbeki had alienated many party members.

Although he prevailed in the rape and initial corruption trials, Zuma continued to face legal challenges. In November 2007, the Supreme Court of Appeal overturned a lower court decision that had made documents seized from Zuma and his lawyer inadmissable in future proceedings. Zuma was expected to go on trial again in August 2008 for racketeering, money laundering, fraud, and corruption, but the date of his trial was postponed. In September, a High Court judge ruled that the case should be thrown out on procedural grounds and suggested in his findings that Mbeki and members of his administration had interfered in the case.

On September 20, 2008, after nine years in office, Thabo Mbeki announced that he had accepted a request by the ANC's National Executive Council to resign as President of South Africa in the wake of the High Court decision. One-third of Mbeki's cabinet resigned with their leader. Among them was Finance Minister Trevor Manuel who, along with Reserve Bank Governor Tito Mboweni, has been widely credited with guiding the country's economic progress since the end of white rule. The inflation rate rose above 13.7%, the highest level since the end of apartheid, amid speculation of Manuel's resignation; he was later reappointed. Other resignations have followed, including that of the Gauteng province premier, who said that he would not be able to "publicly explain or defend the national executive committee's decision on comrade Thabo Mbeki." [9]. The parliament elected

Kgalema Motlanthe, deputy leader of the ANC, as interim President. Motlanthe, a former mine union leader who was imprisoned on Robben Island with Mandela, had recently been appointed by the party as a Member of Parliament, which made him eligible to assume the presidency [10]. Zuma, who did not hold a parliamentary seat, was ineligible to assume the office.

The judge issuing the High Court verdict on which the request for Mbeki's resignation was based made no findings on Zuma's guilt or innocence. Prosecutors filed an appeal, and on January 12, 2009, the Supreme Court of Appeal overturned the High Court ruling. Zuma filed an appeal with the Constitutional Court to have the charges, which he claims are politically motivated, dropped. In March 2008, evidence of collusion between prosecutors, Mbeki, and several senior ANC officials emerged, and, after extensive internal debate, the head of the National Prosecuting Authority (NPA) dropped all charges against Zuma on April 5. Some analysts suggest that the evidence does not affect the merits of the case, and questions have been raised on how that evidence, recorded phone conversations, was obtained. The DA party has strongly criticized the NPA for "grossly inadequate reasons" for its dismissal of Zuma's case [11]. The party has suggested that it will appeal the decision. If Zuma's trial had proceeded and if he were to have been found guilty prior to the elections, he would have been ineligible to become President of South Africa [12].

A New Party Emerges: The Congress of the People

In the wake of Mbeki's resignation, several high-profile ANC figures, including the former Gauteng premier, Mbhazima Shilowa, joined former Defense Minister Mosiuoa Lekota to formally launch a new, centrist political party, the Congress of the People (COPE) in December 2008 [13]. The new party fared well in its first electoral contest, winning a third of the 27 seats in Western Cape municipal by-elections in December [14].

The party maintained momentum in the press in early 2009 with a series of high profile defections from the ANC, including former South African Deputy President Phumzile Mlambo-Ngcuka and businessman Saki Macozoma. COPE has selected Reverend Mvume Dandala as its presidential candidate. Dandala, who has formerly served as Presiding Bishop of the Methodist Church of Southern Africa and as head of the All Africa Council of Churches, is well known for his role in campaigning against apartheid, but has been criticized by the ANC for his relative lack of political experience.

In the party's early months, some analysts suggested that COPE's prospects in the election would be tied to Jacob Zuma's legal challenges. Although the charges against him were dropped, COPE and other opposition parties have publicly maintained that the ANC manipulated the justice system to clear their candidate for the elections.

The April 2009 Elections

South Africans went polls on April 22, 2009, for parliamentary and provincial elections. Approximately 18,000 South Africans living abroad reportedly registered to vote after a court ruling in March 2009 confirmed their right to participate in the elections. They began to cast their ballots on April [15]. In their campaigns, the opposition parties took similar stances on a number of issues. Unlike the ANC, which supports the current electoral system, the opposition advocated for the direct election of the president, provincial premiers, and mayors. The parties also challenged the ANC's decision to disband the country's former elite anti-corruption unit, the Scorpions. Media reports suggested that public disapproval over several recent ANC decisions, such as the government's refusal to issue a visa to the Dalai Lama, could affect voter support for the party. The Dalai Lama had been invited to attend a peace conference in March 2009 along with several other Nobel laureates, who threatened to boycott the event. Some reports suggest pressure from China influenced the government's decision, although government spokesman claims the visa was denied because the Tibetan's visit would have distracted from the World Cup, which was the focus of the conference. Fellow laureate Desmond Tutu was publicly critical, as were opposition leaders and Health Minister Barbara Hogan, who told reporters that the decision implied that the government was "dismissive of human rights."15 Nelson Mandela's grandson, an organizer of the event, suggested that the decision "tainted" South Africa's democratic efforts [16]. The event was postponed [17].

Voter turnout, estimated at 77 percent, was high for the April elections. The ANC maintained its dominance but fell short of retaining its two-thirds majority in the parliament. The ANC now holds 264 seats in the 400-seat assembly, while the main opposition party, the Democratic Alliance (DA), holds 67 seats and gained control of one of the country's nine provinces. COPE received 7.4% of the 2009 vote, picking up 30 seats in the 400-seat parliament, while the Inkatha Freedom Party received acquired only 18 seats.

Jacob Zuma was subsequently chosen by the new parliament to serve as South Africa's newest President. Motlanthe now serves as Deputy President.

Zuma was inaugurated as South Africa's newest President on May 9, 2009, and he named his cabinet the following day. Long-serving Finance Minister Trevor Manuel has been replaced by the well respected former head of South Africa's Revenue Service, Pravin Gordham. Manuel has instead been named to head a new national planning commission that will formulate government strategy. The appointments appear to have allayed market concerns that Zuma would shift the country's economic policy to the left. Secretary of State Hillary Rodham Clinton has welcomed the Zuma government's pledge to continue "a strong economic program" [18]. Health Minister Barbara Hogan has been moved to the Ministry of Public Enterprises, while her replacement, a physician and former provincial official, Aaron Motsoaledi. Businessman and senior ANC member Tokyo Sexwale, who was once considered a possible successor to Mbeki, has been named Minister of Human Settlements. Some analysts believe that his return to politics may signal an interest in vying for the presidency [19]. Jacob Zuma has reportedly vowed to serve only one five-year term.

The Arms Deal and Other Corruption Scandals

The $5.5 billion arms purchase announced by South Africa in 1999 has continued to pose political problems for senior members of the ANC, including Jacob Zuma. Questions remain over the country's need for aircraft, submarines, and surface vessels which were to be acquired under the deal with five European firms. More pressing are allegations of corruption associated with the purchase. Tony Yengeni, the ANC's former chief whip in the National Assembly, was arrested in 2001 on charges of corruption, forgery, and perjury in connection with a large discount he received for the purchase of a luxury car, allegedly in return for assuring that the deal went ahead. He pled guilty to fraud in exchange for acquittal on corruption charges. President Mbeki later fired Deputy President Jacob Zuma, after a judge declared Zuma had a "generally corrupt" relationship with his former financial advisor, Schabir Shaik, who was convicted of fraud and corruption in connection with the arms deal. Zuma was indicted but acquitted in September 2006, after prosecutors failed to build a case against him. Shaik lost an appeal of his conviction in November 2006, when judges ruled that evidence overwhelmingly supported the charge that payments totaling about $165,000 made by Shaik to Zuma were bribes [20]. Shaik was released on medical parole in March 2009. Critics maintain that several questions related to the arms deal remain unresolved, and some are concerned that promised "offsets"—that is, investments by the arms suppliers in South African industry—have not materialized [21]. Former Archbishop Demond Tutu and former South African President F.W. de Klerk have called for a new commission of inquiry to be appointed to investigate the matter.

The local media has also focused attention on the "Travelgate" scandal, in which over thirty current and former members of parliament, most from the ruling ANC party, have appeared in court since 2005 on charges of corruption. Accused of abuse of official travel privileges, the MPs reportedly stole some $3 million in government funds. According to Transparency International, the prosecutions have shown that "the anti-corruption bodies and judiciary have a fair degree of independence and are able to carry out their functions without hindrance, even when high ranking members of the ANC were involved" [22]. More recently, civic activists have raised concern with comments on the judiciary by senior ANC official in relation to the Zuma case [23].

"Travelgate" was followed by another reported scandal popularly referred to as "Oilgate," an allegedly corrupt oil deal between a state-owned oil company and a black economic empowerment company (see below), in which public funds were reportedly illegally diverted into an ANC party campaign fund. To add to the controversy, one of the country's leading newspapers, the Mail and Guardian, was banned by the courts from publishing a report on the scandal. According to media reports, the court ruling found that publishing the report would damage the oil company's right to privacy and was potentially defamatory [24]. The gag order was reportedly the first placed on the paper since apartheid, and was denounced as "an extraordinarily dangerous precedent" to press freedom by the Media Institute for Southern Africa, a press watchdog group.

Several corruption scandals have centered on the country's justice organs themselves. South Africa's chief prosecutor, Vusi Pikoli, was suspended in September 2007 on charges of prosecutorial excess by then-President Mbeki. Many suggest that the subsequent arrest of national police commissioner Jackie Selebi amid allegations that he might have ties to organized crime was directly linked to Pikoli's suspension [25]. Pikoli had been preparing warrants for Selebi's arrest when he was suspended. Selebi, a senior ANC member, is widely considered to be a Mbeki supporter within the party, and some South Africans accused Mbeki of trying to prevent Selebi's arrest. Pikoli was later cleared of wrongdoing, but was not reappointed to his post. Selebi has also been replaced as police commissioner.

The Pikoli and Selebi cases suggest rising political tensions within the country's law enforcement agencies. As chief prosecutor, Pikoli oversaw the Scorpions (the Directorate of Special Operations), South Africa's financial crimes investigative unit. Several leading ANC officials led efforts to have the Scorpions, who have prosecuted several high profile corruption cases, including that of Zuma, disbanded. Zuma and his allies criticized the Scorpions' prosecution of him as politically motivated and suggested in mid-2008 that the Scorpions' duties should be subsumed by the national police. Others, including DA and COPE leaders, argue that the unit's "special status" under the National Prosecuting Authority is needed to tackle corruption at the highest levels. Despite strong opposition from the opposition and civil society, the unit was officially moved by parliament under the authority of the police service in October 2008. Allegations of collusion between Mbeki allies and former heads of both the scorpions and the NPA have raised further questions.

HIV/AIDS

With an estimated 5.7 million South Africans living with HIV in 2007, the country is believed to have the largest AIDS epidemic in the world. According to the Joint United Nations Program on HIV/AIDS (UNAIDS), an estimated 18.1% of South African adults, aged 15-49, were HIV positive that year [26]. UNAIDS also reports that as many as 280,000 children under the age of 15 were HIV positive. AIDS is the leading cause of premature death in South Africa, and the number of AIDS-related deaths there in 2007, some 350,000, was more than double that reported for Nigeria, which has the second highest global mortality figure at 170,000 deaths but almost three times South Africa's population. Approximately 1.4 million children currently living in the country have been orphaned by the disease. As these figures show, the situation is grave.

Thabo Mbeki's stance on HIV/AIDS was a major political issue in South Africa during his tenure. Critics maintain that the former President's ambiguous statements about the disease and lack of leadership on the issue diverted attention and funding from the pandemic at a critical time. In 2000, President Mbeki wrote to then-President Clinton and other heads of state defending dissident scientists who maintain that AIDS is not caused by the HIV virus. In 2001, he rejected appeals that the National Assembly declare the

AIDS pandemic a national emergency. In 2002, President Mbeki drew criticism from the media and others for reportedly insisting that tuberculosis rather than AIDS was the leading cause of death in South Africa, even though the country's Medical Research Council had reported that AIDS was the leading cause, accounting for 40% of mortality among adults aged 15-49 [27]. The reasons for Mbeki's stance on AIDS have been difficult to discern, particularly given that he might have reaped great political advantage from becoming a leader in fighting the epidemic. Some speculate that he feared that AIDS could undermine his vision of South Africa as a leader in an African renaissance sparked by NEPAD and the African Union and thus tended to minimize the importance of the epidemic.

The Mbeki government gradually modified its stance on HIV/AIDS under mounting domestic and international pressure. In 2002, the government announced that it would triple the national AIDS budget, end official opposition to the provision of antiretrovirals for rape victims, and launch a program for universal access to drugs to prevent mother-to-child transmission (MTCT) of HIV. In July 2002, a South African court ordered the government to begin providing the antiretroviral (ARV) drug Nevirapine nationwide to reduce MTCT. The South African Treatment Action Campaign (TAC) had launched the suit in 2001, maintaining that MTCT prevention trials were inadequate and that 20,000 babies could be saved yearly by a nationwide program [28]. At its December 2002 party conference the ANC announced that it was "putting AIDS at the top of our agenda." [29]. The Department of Health in 2003 declared that the government would provide free antiretroviral drugs, but after what observers considered a very slow implementation of the policy, TAC threatened another lawsuit. Under pressure, the government began providing treatment at five hospitals in 2004 and has gradually expanded access to the program. Reports suggest that access to treatment for those with advanced HIV has since increased significantly, from only 4 percent of those in need receiving antiretroviral therapy (ART) in 2004 to 21 percent in 2006 [30].

Despite this commitment by the government to providing ART, many critics still did not consider the Mbeki administration to be serious about the epidemic. In August 2006, then-Health Minister Manto Tshabalala-Msimang drew international criticism for a controversial display of traditional remedies such as garlic, lemons, and beetroot, which she reportedly claimed provided an alternative defense to AIDS, at the International AIDS Conference in Toronto. Stephen Lewis, the U.N. Special Envoy to Africa on AIDS, proclaimed South Africa's AIDS policies as "wrong, immoral, and indefensible" and "worthy of a lunatic fringe" during the conference, and 81 international scientists delivered a petition to Mbeki urging the health minister's dismissal [31]. Many observers consider the Toronto Conference to have prompted a key shift in the government's position. Weeks after the conference, Mbeki appointed his Deputy President, Phumzile Mlambo-Ngcuka, as head of a new national AIDS commission charged with halving the country's infection rate by 2011. She emphasized that the government did believe that HIV causes AIDS and acknowledged "shortcomings" in the government's response to the epidemic. The government also reached out to the AIDS advocacy community, which responded with cautious optimism. TAC, the most vocal critic of the Mbeki Administration's efforts, was cited in late 2006 saying that there was now "a growing enthusiasm, across the board, around the possibility of what we can do as a country in a united fashion" to combat the disease [32]. However, TAC more recently questioned Mbeki's commitment to fighting the epidemic after the August 2007 firing of Tshabalala-Msimang's deputy, who was outspoken about problems with the nation's health services and critical of the Health Minister's controversial views on AIDS.

Although experts believe the country's prevalence rates have begun to stabilize, the South African government still faces many challenges in its response to HIV/AIDS [33]. The emergence of extensively drug resistant tuberculosis (XDR-TB), high rates of HIV/TB co-infection, and significant HIV prevalence rates among health care workers place major strains on the health care system. AIDS activists responded positively to President Motlanthe's appointment of a new health minister, Barbara Hogan.

Land Reform

In order to address historic injustices, the South African government began a land reform program in the late 1990s to restore land rights to those forcibly dispossessed of their land under racially discriminatory apartheid legislation. The government set a number of targets, including the settlement of all land claims [34] by the end of 2008 and the more ambitious transfer of 30% of agricultural lands owned by whites in 1994 to African owners by 2014. While the government's "willing buyer, willing seller" land reform policies have reportedly met with little resistance from white landowners, and the Land Affairs Department reports that almost all land claims have been settled, critics charge that the transfers are going too slowly. According to media reports, the government announced in August 2006 that negotiations with white farmers over the price of land marked for restitution would be limited to six months, after which expropriation could take place if no settlement was reached [35]. Two months later, two white-owned farms claimed by black South Africans were marked for expropriation, a process through which the government would seize the land and pay the owners a price set by independent assessors [36]. This ruling was seen by some analysts as signaling a sense of urgency on the part of the government to speed up reforms.

In a 2005 speech on the perceived slow pace of land transfers, then-Deputy President MlamboNgcuka said that South Africa might learn from Zimbabwe's land reform process, igniting considerable controversy. President Mbeki dismissed critics of the speech, saying the Deputy President's words were misinterpreted and that Zimbabwe's policies were only one among many the government had studied. The media reported a similarly controversial discussion document circulated by the Land Affairs Department suggesting replacing the "willing buyer, willing seller" approach with a "Zimbabwean model," or forced-sale principle (Zimbabwe's policy that preceded the country's land invasions). Under this proposed model, farmers who want to sell their land must offer the government the right of first refusal. If they refused a government offer, they could not sell the land on the open market. The discussion paper was said to propose the expropriation of commercial agricultural land to meet the government's target of 30% redistribution. At that time, government officials stressed that the document was for internal discussion only and did not reflect official policy [37].

In 2008, the Mbeki Administration appeared determined to speed up the transfer of commercial agricultural lands. Official figures suggest that the government has met only 5% of its 30% target for state-funded transfers, and the Land Affairs Department suggests that sellers are demanding excessively high prices. The government tabled legislation before parliament in July that would accelerate the process by adding a constitutional provision for expropriation of a property "for a public purpose." Critics, including the Democratic Alliance, argued that the proposed law, which would restrict property owners' rights to judicial appeal and force sales at below market prices, would undermine confidence in property rights and deter investment [38]. They also suggest that while the rate of state-funded transfers has been slow, substantial transfers have been made privately through the property market. The legislation was shelved, but some speculate that it will be resubmitted. In March 2008, the government introduced a controversial new "use it or lose it" initiative that allows farms that have been transferred to black beneficiaries to be taken by the government if they are deemed unproductive.

In a 2004 survey of South Africans of all races, 72% of black respondents agreed with the statement: “All the land whites own, they stole from blacks” [39]. According to an independent South African think tank,

> The most universal and immediate land need in South Africa is for ‘a place to stay’ rather than ‘a place to farm’.... Even among employed agricultural workers, land demand is modest. Among people living on the land without alternative sources of income, however, aspirations for land or more land can reach high levels, and become very intense. Although this is a minority group, it is large in numerical terms, and hence constitutes a significant policy challenge [40].

The targets for reform set by the ANC government have set public expectations high, and some analysts suggest that the perceived pace of land reform may be an issue in the 2009 elections.

Crime

As South Africa prepares to host hundreds of thousands of tourists during the soccer World Cup in 2010, the government continues to battle perceptions that the country is not safe for tourists because of its high crime rate. According to one survey, one-third of potential tourists have been deterred from visiting South Africa out of fear of becoming victim to a criminal act [41]. Some analysts attribute the high rate of crime to the country’s high level of wealth disparity, but also to shortcomings within the police force and in the lack of a comprehensive government approach. South African officials have acknowledged the problem. In February 2007, then-President Mbeki admitted crime had created a high level of fear around the country, and the South African Safety and Security Minister called the high number of cases of violent crime “disconcerting and unacceptable” [42]. The government plans to recruit 30,000 new police officers before the games.

The Economy

South Africa won praise from international economists for its reform-oriented macro-economic policy in the late 1990s, which, according to the U.S. Department of Commerce, "demonstrated its commitment to open markets, privatization, and a favorable investment climate, moving away from the former government's strategy of import substitution and industrial development that protected local industries with high tariff barriers" [43]. The policy, known as the Growth, Employment and Redistribution (GEAR) strategy, delivered mixed results—it engendered macroeconomic stability, fiscal discipline, and trade liberalization. However, unemployment continued to rise, and income distribution did not show signs of significant improvement. Nevertheless, the income of the average black household almost doubled in the first decade after the end of apartheid [44].

The rate of growth in Gross Domestic Product (GDP) averaged 3% per year in the first decade after apartheid and rose to an average of 5% from 2004 to 2007. The growth rate fell to an estimated 3.2% in 2008, due in part to the global economic downturn, and is expected to decrease to 1.2% in 2009 before rising above 3% again in 2010 [45]. Much higher growth rates will be needed if South Africa is to substantially increase employment among the black majority and reduce the sharp inequalities in income distribution among the races. Unemployment estimates range from 25% to 40%, far above the government's target of 15%. The vast, poverty-stricken townships surrounding South Africa's cities remain a potential source of political instability. In recent years periodic riots have erupted in several poor municipalities to protest local government corruption and inadequate service delivery. Although turnout and support for the ANC remained high nationally in the country's last nationwide municipal elections, voters boycotted the polls in a number of townships in which the ANC had formerly enjoyed strong support, and several hundred former ANC supporters stood as independent candidates. Conditions in the townships have improved marginally with the expanded availability of electricity and the provision of clean water taps. However, popular resentment is reportedly deepening with respect to the widening gap between the rich and poor.

Some economists attribute South Africa's economic difficulties, in part, to the slow pace of privatization. Despite its commitment to privatization, the government remains heavily involved in transportation, communications, energy production, and the defense sector, and after the 2004 elections expressed a desire to restructure most remaining state-owned enterprises rather than expand privatization. Delays are due partly to government concerns that privatization will boost unemployment temporarily, fueling criticism from COSATU and the SACP. Moreover, the government is trying to find ways to promote "black empowerment" by assuring that a significant portion of the shares in privatized companies will be acquired by black South Africans rather than by wealthy whites or foreign investors. Another point of view, championed by COSATU and the SACP, is that job cutbacks that often follow privatization are contributing to unemployment and the growing income gap in South Africa. Some argue that the government should intervene in the economy to save jobs, and to create new jobs, perhaps through a major public works program.

In 2005, the government unveiled its new Accelerated and Shared Growth Initiative for South Africa (ASGISA), which is designed to raise the average economic growth rate to 4.5% from 2004-2009 and to at least 6% from 2010-1014 through targeted interventions, including public investment in infrastructure. The ASGISA plan also aims, through these economic growth policies, to cut unemployment rates in half by 2014; some experts consider these targets impossible for the country to meet [46]. Another economic program, the government's Black Economic Empowerment (BEE) program, was initiated in 1994 and is designed to address racial inequalities in the business sector. In 1994, blacks owned less than 5% of the country's private enterprises. As of mid-2008 there were over 15 black-owned and 29 black-empowered companies listed on the South African stock exchange. The rise in black ownership has been echoed by a significant increase in the black middle class. Nevertheless, the lack of skilled labor may be hampering the success of the program, as may complicated or unclear regulations. According to a 2005 survey of domestic and foreign firms, "While supporting the need for affirmative action, most foreign investors acknowledge that the lack of clarity surrounding the application of Black Economic Empowerment has had a dampening effect on their plans to further invest in South Africa" [47].

In February 2007, the government instituted the BEE Codes of Good Practice, which make both listed and unlisted companies subject to empowerment requirements and targets, but offers concessions to small businesses and foreign investors [48]. In September 2007, Sasol, the country's oil and coal company, announced its intention to transfer 10% of the company to black owners to qualify under BEE rules.

In the first decade of post-apartheid rule, analysts expressed concern over the government's ability to attract foreign investment at the levels needed to spur growth. Sound macroeconomic policies, including reduced tariffs and export subsidies, the loosening of exchange controls, improved enforcement of intellectual property laws, and legislation designed to improve competition have been cited by observers as responsible for the country's economic growth. A World Bank study found that South Africa is one of the top 35 easiest countries in which to do business [49]. Investors are, however, reportedly worried by labor relations, high crime rates, and corruption. Transparency International ranks South Africa 54 out of 158 in its 2008 Corruption Perceptions Index, indicating that it is perceived as less corrupt than other Sub-Saharan African countries (only three African countries ranked less corrupt than South Africa), but more corrupt than many competitors for investment in other parts of the world [50]. Its ranking fell from 43 in 2007. Political risks arising from regional instability, particularly in Zimbabwe, are regarded as another deterrent to investors, and South Africa's own racial, class, and political divisions are seen as sources of concern. The resignation of President Mbeki shook investor confidence. Some studies suggest that business confidence is at it lowest level in five years, due in part to instability in the global financial markets but also because of concerns regarding in-fighting within the ANC [51].

As Africa's largest economy, South Africa has been affected by the recent global economic downturn, and its retail, mining, and manufacturing sectors have declined. Economists warn that South Africa's unemployment rate could rise in 2009, with the country losing up to 300,000 jobs [52]. As discussed above, however, the economy is expected to rebound in 2010. Some analysts have highlighted the country's executive "brain drain" as one of greatest threats to South Africa's economic progress. They also suggest that the outcome of the debate over the role of state assistance may have the greatest effect on the country's capability to meet ASGISA goals.

Electricity Shortages

The country's continued economic growth is also threatened by an overstretched electricity network. In January 2008, South Africans experienced severe electrical power cuts throughout the country. Estimates indicate that the cuts may have cost the economy millions [53]. The crucial mining sector was hit particularly hard, causing global gold and platinum prices to rise. Many mines closed for several days as the power cuts threatened worker safety. Electricity from South Africa was also temporarily cut to neighboring countries. State-owned Eskom, the world's fourth largest power company, and the Mbeki Administration blamed one another for the crisis. The government has begun rationing electricity and is accelerating plans to build new power plants and rehabilitate old ones. Experts suggest the shortages may nevertheless continue for several years, and consumers have faced steep increases in their power bills [54].

U.S. Relations

U.S. policies toward South Africa and the anti-apartheid struggle were a contentious issue from the 1960s through the 1980s, with many arguing that the United States was doing too little to promote human rights and democratic rule. Congress enacted the Comprehensive Anti-Apartheid Act of 1986 (P.L. 99-440) over President Reagan's veto in order to affirm U.S. support for democratic change. The legislation imposed a number of sanctions against South Africa. The Reagan Administration, by contrast, had been pursuing a policy of "constructive engagement" (i.e., dialogue) with the white South African regime, regarding this approach as the most effective way of promoting change.

In the early 1990s, the United States assumed a lead role in supporting South Africa's transition to democracy. Policy makers at that time saw the South African democratization process as a model for other African countries, and expected that the country would soon become a stabilizing force as well as an engine for economic growth throughout the sub-Saharan region. South Africa's need to focus on domestic economic and social problems meant that U.S. expectations for the country's regional role were perhaps not met in full in the first post-apartheid years. But South Africa's leadership in the launching of NEPAD; the deployment of South African peacekeepers to Burundi, Cote d'Ivoire, and Sudan; and intensive South African involvement in the peace process in the Democratic Republic of the Congo have highlighted South Africa's capabilities as a regional actor. South Africa also assisted U.S. efforts to resolve the Haiti crisis by providing an exile location for former President Bertrand Aristide. Given South Africa's role in conflict mediation and resolution throughout the continent, the United States has worked to expand the country's peacekeeping abilities through the African Contingency Operations Training Assistance (ACOTA) program [55].

Since 1992, South Africa has been among the leading African recipients of U.S. aid. U.S. assistance to South Africa has increased in recent years, rising from an estimated $224 million in FY2006, to $398 million in FY2007.

The Bush Administration obligated an estimated $574 million for FY2008, and requested almost $576 million for FY2009.56 In its FY2008 congressional budget justification, the State Department reported that "the U.S. Government's (USG) relationship with South Africa is transforming from that of donor to one of strategic partnership," and accordingly, "activities in Peace and Security will continue to increase in importance while development programs will be phased out in the next couple of years." U.S. assistance will continue to focus on fighting HIV/AIDS and tuberculosis and assisting the South African government to implement economic reforms and to improve its regional peacekeeping capacity. USAID programs have supported efforts to promote sound governance, reduce unemployment and poverty, increase access to shelter and basic municipal services, and improve the quality of education and the country's health system. U.S. assistance includes $850,000 in International Military Education and Training (IMET) programs in South Africa.

The United States provides significant assistance to South Africa's fight against HIV/AIDS through the President's Emergency Plan for AIDS Relief (PEPFAR), having contributed over $1,447 million since the program's inception in FY2004. The Bush Administration requested $557 million for FY2009 through the Global HIV/AIDS Initiative. By the end of FY2008, the PEPFAR program had provided ARV therapy to an estimated 549,700 patients, transmission prevention treatment to over 462,400 pregnant HIV-infected women, and palliative and/or tuberculosis care for 1,852,700 South Africans. PEPFAR's South Africa program also funds public education efforts to promote abstinence, faithfulness, and healthy behavior to reduce the risk of transmission among high-risk groups.

The 110th Congress took steps to address lingering restrictions on U.S. visas for members of the ANC, including former Presidents Mbeki and Mandela, who were convicted under the previous apartheid government of crimes against that regime. In May 2008, the House of Representatives passed H.R. 5690, sponsored by House Foreign Affairs Committee Chairman Howard Berman. The legislation removed the ANC from treatment as a terrorist organization, instructed U.S. government agencies to remove any terrorist designations regarding the ANC and its leaders from their databases, and gave discretion to the State and Homeland Security Departments in determining admissibility of visa applicants based upon specified criminal convictions or terrorist activities undertaken in opposition to apartheid rule. Secretary of State Condoleeza Rice called the restrictions "embarassing" [57]. Senator John Kerry introduced companion legislation, S. 2979. Members of the 110th

Congress also introduced legislation honoring Mandela, H.Res. 1090, and Archbishop Desmond Tutu, H.Res. 34.

Cooperation in Fighting Terrorism

U.S. and South African law enforcement authorities have cooperated for several years on terrorism investigations, including investigations into the possibility that South Africa has been used as a haven for Islamic militants from outside the region [58]. In 1999, South African authorities arrested Khalfan Khamis Mohamed, a Tanzanian later convicted in the bombing of the U.S. embassy in Dar es Salaam, and deported him to the United States. Khalfan had reportedly sought to hide among Cape Town's Muslims after he fled Tanzania. More recently, one of the suspects of the 2005 London bombings, Haroon Rashid Aswat, who was arrested in Zambia, was thought to have spent time in South Africa. There is continuing concern that other terrorists may seek to hide in South Africa, or make use of its modern transportation and communications systems for transit, smuggling, and money-laundering [59].

The U.S. Department of Treasury's Office of Foreign Assets Control (OFAC) includes several South African nationals in its Specially Designated Nationals List (SDN), which sanctions individuals and groups believed to have links to terrorism. In a controversial move, the South African government used its position in 2007 as a member of the U.N. Security Council's Al-Qaeda and Taliban Sanctions Committee, also known as the 1276 Committee, to block United Nations travel and financial sanctions on two of these individuals, Farhad Ahmed Dockrat and Dr. Junaid Ismail Dockrat. The South African government argued that it required more time to examine the evidence against the Dockrats before applying sanctions.

There is concern over the potential use of South African travel documents by would-be terrorists. At the time of his arrest, Haroon Rashid Aswat was carrying a South African passport, and according to media reports, others with suspected ties to terrorism have been apprehended at U.S. and British borders, as well as in Pakistan, with South African travel documents [60]. The U.S. State Department's Office of the Coordinator for Counterterrorism has noted concern regarding fraudulent travel documents, saying, "efforts to limit the accessibility of passports and identity documents to potential terrorists are limited by resources and corruption in the Department of Home Affairs" [61]. South African passports were found during raids by British police on suspected terror groups in London in 2004 and 2005. South Africa's intelligence minister reported in August 2005 that groups allegedly linked to al-Qaeda had been discovered in southern Africa and that maritime targets could be threatened. U.S. law enforcement agencies provide training to their South African counterparts, supply needed equipment to the South Africa Police Service, and share information [62].

The South African government has expressed differences with the United States in the latter's designation of Hamas and Hezbollah as terrorist organizations. In May 2007, prior to the Hamas military seizure of the Gaza Strip, the South African Minister of Intelligence met with Hamas leader and then-Prime Minister of the Palestinian Authority Ismail Haniyeh. According to some media reports, he publically praised Hamas and invited Haniyeh to visit South Africa.

Diplomatic Differences

Despite the cordial relations that officially exist between South Africa and the United States, some analysts suggest that diplomatic differences highlight what former U.S. Assistant Secretary of State for African Affairs Jendayi Frazer referred to as a "rough patch" in U.S.-South African relations [63].

As one U.S. official pointed out, the country has had close ties with the Non-Aligned Movement countries, and has exhibited "marked sympathy toward countries that exert their independence from the West" [64]. Some South African officials expressed opposition to the Bush Administration's initial proposal to locate the new U.S. combatant command, Africa Command or AFRICOM, on the continent [65]. However, the government later allowed a historic visit by a U.S. aircraft carrier, the USS Theodore Roosevelt, in October 2008, and military relations are reportedly improving. South Africa has taken a critical stance toward the war in Iraq, and former President Nelson Mandela has been vocal in his opposition to what he views as U.S. unilateralism on Iraq. South Africa has also differed significantly with the United States on Iran. During an 2006 visit by the Iranian Foreign Minister to Pretoria, South Africa affirmed its support for Iran's "inalienable right to pursue nuclear energy for peaceful purposes," at the same time that the Mbeki government announced its intention to consider renewing its uranium enrichment program [66]. South Africa, which dismantled its own nuclear weapons program after the fall of apartheid, insisted that any enrichment program would be strictly peaceful in nature.

The United Nations

South Africa's recent role as a non-permanent member of the U.N. Security Council was controversial, and the South African government has been criticized by the United States as well as by many human rights activists for its lack of support for human rights issues raised before the Council [67]. In January 2007, South Africa voted against a resolution on political prisoners in Burma, arguing that alleged human rights abuses in sovereign countries are not covered by the mandate of the Security Council as defined by the U.N. Charter. It argued that because the abuses do not pose a direct threat to international peace and security, they would be more appropriately addressed by the U.N. Human Rights Council [68]. In March 2007, while serving a one-month term as President of the Security Council, South Africa reportedly blocked discussion of human rights abuses in Zimbabwe [69]. Nobel laureate Archbishop Desmond Tutu said of the Burma vote, in which China and Russia cast a double veto, "I am deeply disappointed by our vote. It is a betrayal of our own noble past. The tyrannical military regime is gloating, and we sided with them. If others had used the arguments we are using today when we asked them for their support against apartheid, we might still have been unfree," [70]. Former DA leader Tony Leon expressed similar sentiments on his government's alleged refusal to address the Zimbabwe situation, calling it "extraordinary irony" that the ANC government would use the same argument used to block debate on the abuses of the former apartheid regime in South Africa [71].

In July 2008, South Africa voted with Russia, China, Vietnam, and Libya in opposition to a U.S.- sponsored resolution on Zimbabwe (S/2008/447) that called for targeted sanctions on select members of the Mugabe regime, an international arms embargo, the appointment of a U.N. Special Representative on Zimbabwe, and the creation of a Panel of Experts to monitor and evaluate the situation and the effects of the sanctions.

South Africa and the United States also differed on Middle East issues addressed by the Security Council. In May 2007, South Africa abstained from a U.S.-sponsored resolution to establish an international tribunal to investigate political killings in Lebanon, arguing that although it supported a tribunal with "Lebanese ownership," it was not appropriate for the Security Council to impose a tribunal upon the country and "politicize international criminal law" [72]. The country was vocal in its opposition to Security Council sanctions on both Sudan and Iran, arguing that such sanctions would ultimately harden the target governments' positions rather than reduce tensions. However, after efforts to modify resolution language, South Africa ultimately did vote for sanctions against Iran in March 2007, "to remind Iran of its responsibility towards the IAEA and the Nonproliferation Treaty" [73].

Zimbabwe [74]

Political and economic turmoil in neighboring Zimbabwe has led to a massive exodus of Zimbabweans in search of work. A recent nationwide outbreak of cholera in Zimbabwe exacerbated the flight. Some sources estimate that as many as four million Zimbabweans (30% of the total population) are now living outside the country. South African government sources reported a sharp increase in border crossings after the Zimbabwean government implemented price controls on basic commodities in June 2007. Zimbabwe's other neighbors, Zambia, Botswana, and Mozambique, also have seen a significant rise in immigration in the last year. While many stay in these countries to look for work or stay with relatives, others commute across the border daily to buy basic staples that have been unavailable in their own country. Those who were caught by South African police have been sent back to Zimbabwe; the International Organization for Migration (IOM) reported that the number of Zimbabweans repatriated from its facility in Beitbridge, South Africa increased from 40,000 in the last six months of 2006 to almost 118,000 in the first six months of 2007. The government recently changed its immigration policy for Zimbabweans, allowing them to receive temporary visitors' permits.

As mentioned above, tensions over perceived competition for resources led in May 2008 to xenophobic attacks on Zimbabweans and other immigrants in townships throughout South Africa. Many were rendered homeless and forced to seek shelter in temporary camps established by the South African government, while others chose to return to their country of origin. Cases of cholera have been reported in South Africa and other neighboring countries.

During his 2003 visit to Africa, President George W. Bush called then-President Mbeki his "point man" on Zimbabwe [75]. The United States has been outspoken in its criticism of the policies of Zimbabwe's President Robert Mugabe with respect to human rights, democracy, and land reform, and has imposed "targeted sanctions" prohibiting travel to the United States by Zimbabwe leaders. President Mbeki, by contrast, chose to deal with President Mugabe through "quiet diplomacy," or diplomatic engagement, and South African officials have called for western countries to reconsider the penalties they have imposed on Zimbabwe.

As Zimbabwe's largest trading partner, many observers have considered South Africa to be in a position to exert substantial leverage on its neighbor.

At the same time, South Africa must weigh the unintended effects of such leverage—state collapse across its northern border could produce a sharp increase in illegal migration and have a substantial impact on South Africa. In 2005, as the International Monetary Fund (IMF) threatened to expel Zimbabwe from the Fund for debt payment arrears, the country requested a loan of up to $1 billion from South Africa for fuel, food, and electricity, as well as to address the IMF payments. Amid rumors that the South African government would make any potential loan conditional on economic and political reforms, the loan negotiations stalled and Mugabe found another source from which to repay the IMF dues [76].

In March 2007, Southern African Development Community (SADC) leaders appointed President Mbeki to mediate between the Zimbabwean government and the opposition. In June 2007, South Africa initiated talks between the Mugabe Administration, represented by the country's Ministers of Labor and Justice, and the two MDC factions, represented by their respective Secretary-Generals, in Pretoria. President Mugabe's proclamation in January 2008 that national elections would be held on March 29, 2008, while opposition rallies in the country continued to be suppressed by police, angered the opposition and led to the dialogue's collapse.

Following Zimbabwe's 2005 parliamentary elections, which the British and American governments termed "fundamentally flawed" and "seriously tainted," the head of South Africa's parliamentary observer mission, Mbulelo Goniwe, chief whip of the ruling African National Congress (ANC), was quoted saying that the delegation had "unanimously agreed that the elections were credible, legitimate, free and fair" [77]. Leading the Southern African Development Community (SADC) observer delegation, then-South African Deputy President Mlambo-Ngcuka congratulated Zimbabwe on "the holding of a peaceful, credible, well-managed and transparent election. The people of Zimbabwe have expressed their will in an impressively instructive manner that will go a long way in contributing to the consolidation of democracy and political stability not only in Zimbabwe, but also in the region as a whole."78 Both statements received substantial criticism in the international press.

Mbeki's Zimbabwe policies drew criticism from within his country; former President Mandela, Archbishop Tutu, former opposition leader Tony Leon, and even the ANC's ally, the Congress of South African Trade Unions (COSATU), have been vocal detractors. COSATU delegations have been forcibly expelled from Zimbabwe twice, first in 2004 and later in 2006, when COSATU members traveled to Harare to express their support for Zimbabwean human rights activists after incidents of alleged police violence.

One COSATU leader remarked, "we are not quiet diplomats," and "we will not keep mum when freedom does not lead to respect for workers and human rights" [79]. When the Mbeki government issued a terse initial statement following the March 11, 2007, arrest of opposition and civil society activists, COSATU criticized the government for a "disgraceful" response, "in the face of such massive attacks on democracy and human rights, especially coming from those who owed so much to international solidarity when South Africans were fighting for democracy and human rights against the apartheid regime" [80].

Jacob Zuma has previously referred to the Zimbabwean president as "a monster," but he has also defended Mbeki's quiet diplomacy [81]. Other ANC heavyweights like Cyril Ramaphosa and Tokyo Sexwale criticized Mbeki's policy. Sexwale has said, "When a freedom fighter takes a wrong step, it is time for other freedom fighters to stand up and say 'we know you are a great man, but we cannot support what you are doing'" [82]. In 2007, he suggested that the Zimbabwean government might be ignoring Mbeki's efforts, and that it might be time to "turn up the volume [83]. Ramaphosa expressed similar sentiments.

President Mbeki's reluctance to take a more critical stance toward the Mugabe Administration led to increasing calls for the South African leader to be replaced as the SADC mediator on Zimbabwe. Tsvangirai criticized Mbeki for his "quiet support for the dictatorship," and has called for him to step down as mediator [84]. According to reports, President Mbeki recently wrote President Bush a letter warning the United States not to interfere in the Zimbabwe situation [85]. But as the violence increased after the 2008 elections in Zimbabwe, public and internal ANC pressure may have forced Mbeki to take a stronger position with President Mugabe. Mbeki visited Zimbabwe on several occasions after the elections, and he dispatched six retired generals to investigate reports of attacks on the opposition. The generals reportedly expressed shock at the level of violence [86]. Under Mbeki's mediation, the Zimbabwe parties reconvened for talks in South Africa, and on September 15, 2008, after several weeks of negotiations, Mugabe and MDC leader Morgan Tsvangirai signed a power-sharing arrangement aimed at resolving the political standoff. After a four month delay, the parties reached agreement on several key implementation details and Tsvangirai become Prime Minister of a new coalition government. Cabinet positions have been divided among the parties. Like other international donors, the United States has expressed cautious support for the new arrangement, but has reaffirmed that certain conditions must be met before non-humanitarian assistance to the government will resume. For more information, see CRS Report RL34509, Zimbabwe: The Power Sharing Agreement and Implications for U.S. Policy, by Lauren Ploch.

Trade

The United States and South Africa enjoy a strong trade relationship. As Table 1 indicates, the United States runs a deficit in its merchandise trade with South Africa.

Table 1. U.S. Merchandise Trade with South Africa ($ billions)

	2003	2004	2005	2006	2007
Exports to South Africa	2.819	3.178	3.907	4.462	5.518
Imports from South Africa	4.624	5.945	5.886	7.501	9.075
Balance	- 1.805	-2.766	- 1.979	-3.039	-3.557

Source: U.S. Census Bureau, Foreign Trade Division.

Nevertheless, South Africa is the largest market for U.S. goods on the continent, with imports totaling over $5.5 billion in 2007. Leading U.S. exports include transportation equipment, chemicals, and electronic products, while leading imports include minerals and metals, and transportation equipment [87]. U.S. officials point out that South Africa continues to enjoy major benefits from the African Growth and Opportunity Act (AGOA, P.L. 106-200), enacted by Congress in May 2000, with nearly all of the country's exports qualifying for duty-free entry into the United States. Through AGOA, South Africa exported $2.3 billion in such products as vehicles, chemicals, minerals, metals, and agricultural, textile, and apparel products in 2007, making the country the largest and most diversified supplier of non-fuel products under AGOA.

During a 2002 visit to South Africa, U.S. Trade Representative Robert Zoellick proposed the creation of the United States' first free trade agreement (FTA) with sub-Saharan Africa, linking the United States with South Africa and the other members of the Southern Africa Customs Union (SACU): Botswana, Lesotho, Swaziland, and Namibia. SACU is the United States' second largest trading partner in Africa behind petroleum-rich Nigeria. Reaction to the FTA proposal in the region was reportedly positive, but there were concerns about the scope of the negotiations. Some observers felt that

U.S. proposals to include intellectual property, government procurement, and services in the negotiations could have a negative impact on the SACU countries, and that the United States was not sensitive to the differing levels of development within SACU. Negotiations began in 2003 but were suspended in 2006, when U.S. and SACU officials agreed on a new work program that will aim to address a broad range of trade and investment issues, and may contribute in the long term toward a possible FTA. Analysts suggest that the momentum for SACU negotiators to complete the FTA may have been lost, given that AGOA benefits were extended through the AGOA Acceleration Act of 2004 (P.L. 108-274) until 2015 [88].

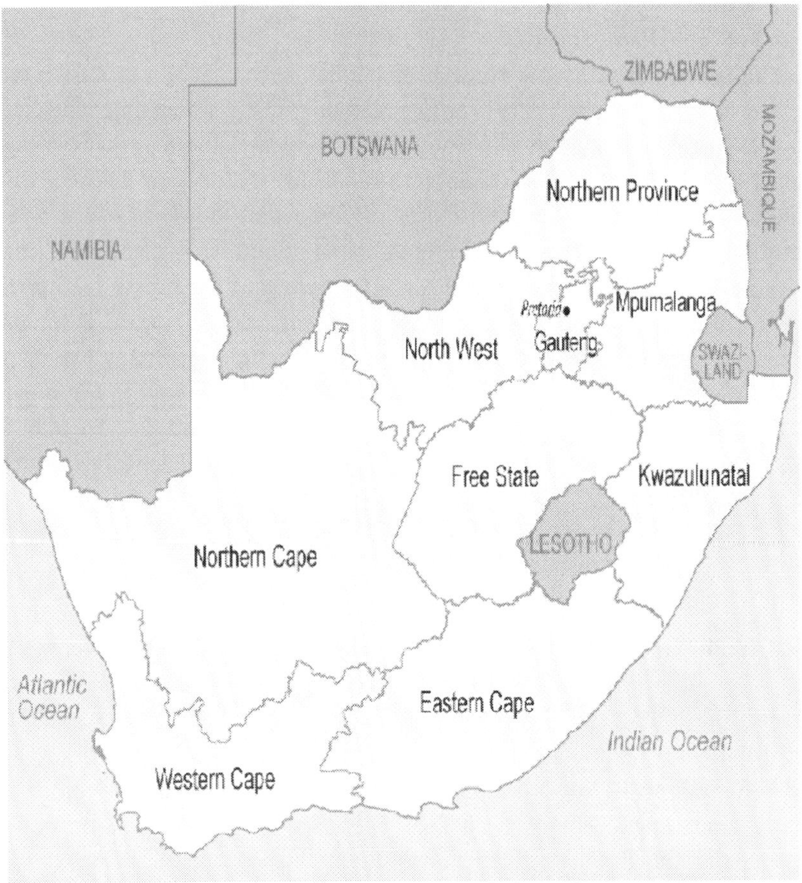

Note: South Africa highlighted; all shaded areas are independent countries.

Figure 1. Map of South Africa's Provinces.

Prospects for the Future

Analysts seem generally confident that South Africa will remain politically stable for some time to come. There are tensions in rural areas over land, but South Africa seems far from a rural upheaval over the issue, as has been the case in Zimbabwe. Social tensions over perceived inequalities in the distribution of wealth and inadequate service delivery, which resulted in violent attacks on African immigrants in mid-2008, are likely to continue in the near term as the government struggles to address the needs of its poorest citizens. South Africa's longer term stability is linked to the success of the South African government and its partners in fighting poverty and reducing the toll of the AIDS pandemic.

The principal worry for some analysts has been that South Africa would become a de facto one- party state under the ANC, weakening checks and balances in the political system. Should this happen, some fear that the regime could become increasingly authoritarian and unresponsive to the needs of its citizens. ANC leaders reject this view, arguing that their party is a national liberation movement committed to transforming South Africa and fulfilling the aspirations of the poor [89]. Others have argued that the power of the ruling party is limited by the country's free and very active press, independent judiciary, and a bill of rights enshrined in the constitution. In any event, ANC leaders want their country to be seen as a leader in Africa, and as a spokesman for Africa and developing countries generally in world affairs. To play such roles, South Africa must continue to be recognized as a successful democracy.

References

[1] South Africa's involvement in AMIS was not without controversy. Some opposition leaders criticized Mbeki for not taking a more assertive role in the crisis, and some South African troops threatened to pull out of AMIS in late 2006 over a pay dispute.

[2] "Sanctions Threat on Sudan Counterproductive: South Africa," *Agence France Presse*, June 21, 2007.

[3] Under the South African constitution, the President is elected by the National Assembly, and consequently, the next President is likely to be chosen from the majority ANC party.

[4] Tom Lodge, "The Future of South Africa's Party System," *Journal of Democracy,* Vol 17, No. 3, July 2006, p. 154.

[5] In November 2002, Mbeki named two NNP figures to positions as deputy ministers in his government. "Mbeki Gives Van Schalkwyk Space with New Positions," *Business Day*, November 5, 2002.

[6] "South Africa: Balanced Opposition," *Business Day,* April 26, 2007.

[7] "Mbeki, Nzimande Clash Over Splits in Alliance," *Business Day*, October 9, 2006.

[8] "S Africa Unions Call Off Strike," *BBC*, June 28, 2007.

[9] "Manuel Plays Down Chance of ANC Split," *Mail and Guardian,* September 30, 2008.

[10] In South Africa, parties make appointments to fill vacant parliamentary seats, rather than holding by-elections. Motlanthe was appointed as a member of parliament in May 2008 and was appointed to Mbeki's cabinet in July 2008 as a Minister without Portfolio.

[11] "DA Slams Dismissal of Probe into 'Mbekigate' Tapes," *Mail and Guardian*, March 31, 2009.

[12] South Africa's constitution requires elections to be held within 90 days of the expiration of the National Assembly's five year term, on April 13, 2009. The new Assembly will choose the president after they are seated.

[13] The ANC has challenged the party's name in court.

[14] The ANC is challenging a ruling by the Electoral Commission that barred party candidates from standing in 12 of the 27 constituencies.

[15] "Govt: Hogan's Dalai Lama Comments 'Unfortunate,'" *Mail and Guardian,* March 25, 2009.

[16] "S. Africans Angered by Decision to Deny Visa to Dalai Lama," *Washington Post*, March 24, 2009.

[17] President Zuma's new Foreign Minister has reportedly announced that the Dalai Lama is now welcome to visit South Africa at any time.

[18] Secretary of State Hillary Rodham Clinton Interview With Manelisi Dubase of South African Broadcasting Corporation, May 19, 2009.

[19] "Zuma Calms Markets with New Cabinet," BBC, May 10, 2009.

[20] Shaik was released on medical parole in March 2009.

[21] "The Arms Deal—The Shadows Lengthen," *Business Day*, September 20, 2006; "SA Laureates Demand Arms Inquiry," BBC, December 4, 2008.

[22] Berlin-based Transparency International (TI) describes itself as a non-governmental organization devoted to combating corruption. TI, *Global Corruption Report 2006.*

[23] "Judiciary Should be Protected from Scandalous Commentary," *Pretoria News,* July 11, 2008.

[24] The Media Institute of Southern Africa, "Media Freedom Has 'Suffered Major Blow,'" May 28, 2005.

[25] See, for example, "Lets All Arrest One Another," *The Economist,* January 17, 2008 and "Party Power Struggle Enthralls South Africa," New York Times, October 12, 2007.

[26] UNAIDS, *2008 Report on the Global AIDS Epidemic*, August 2008.

[27] "South Africa President Mbeki Criticizes U.N. AIDS Fund Grant," *Associated Press,* July 25, 2002, and "Research Affirms Disease Is Nation's Leading Cause of Death," *The Washington Post,* October 19, 2001.

[28] "AIDS Activists Sue South Africa," *Associated Press*, August 21, 2001.

[29] *Reuters.* President Mbeki was criticized by some, however, for not giving the AIDS epidemic greater prominence in his address to the conference.

[30] UNAIDS, *2008 Report on the Global AIDS Epidemic*, August 2008.

[31] The letter, titled "Expression of Concern by HIV Scientists," can be found at http://www.aidstruth.org/letter-tombeki.php. See also "Under Fire, South Africa Shakes Up Its Strategy Against AIDS," The New York Times, September 3, 2006, and "In South Africa, a Dramatic Shift on AIDS; Treatment, Prevention Get New Emphasis as Deputy President Takes Key Role," *The Washington Post*, October 27, 2006.

[32] "Under Fire, South Africa Shakes Up Its Strategy Against AIDS," *The New York Times,* September 3, 2006.

[33] The Henry J. Kaiser Family Foundation, "HIV/AIDS Policy Fact Sheet," October 2008.

[34] Black citizens have filed over 79,700 land claims since January 1999, according to a report by Michael Wines, "South Africa to Seize Two White-Owned Farms," *New York Times,* October 10, 2006.

[35] "ANC Gives Ultimatum to White Farmers," *The Daily Telegraph*, August 14, 2006.

[36] "South Africa to Seize Two White-Owned Farms, *New York Times,* October 10, 2006.

[37] "'Zimbabwe' Land Option Mooted by Officials," *Business Day,* October 16, 2006.

[38] "Expropriation Must Be a Land Resort," *Business Day*, May 30, 2008.

[39] In a survey of 3500 respondents 2004, South Africans were asked to respond to the statement: "All the land whites own, they stole from the

blacks." and were asked to present their responses in a range, from "strongly agree" to "strongly disagree." Over 72% responded "strongly agree" or "agree." Cited in "Land Issue Illustrates Social Rift," *Business Day,* 5 May 2004.

[40] The Centre for Development and Enterprise, *Land Reform in South Africa: a* 21st *Century Perspective,* Johannesburg: June 2005, p. 30.

[41] "Crime 'Deters' SA 2010 Tourists," *BBC*, July 23, 2007.

[42] "SA Violent Crime 'Unacceptable,'" *BBC*, July 3, 2007.

[43] U.S. Department of Commerce, *South Africa Country Commercial Guide, Fiscal Year 2003*, July 2002.

[44] The average household income for blacks increased by 71% from 1996 to 2004, according to the South African Institute for Race Relations' *South Africa Survey 2004/2005.*

[45] The Economist Intelligence Unit (EIU), *Country Report: South Africa*, December 2008.

[46] EIU, December 2008.

[47] United States Department of Commerce, "Doing Business in South Africa: A Country Commercial Guide for U.S. Companies," 2006.

[48] Multinational corporations can maintain 100% ownership provided they meet other BEE criteria, including employment and procurement targets.

[49] The country rose from a ranking of 35 in 2008 to 32 in 2009. See the *Doing Business* section of the World Bank's website at http://www.worldbank.org.

[50] The Transparency International index is based on the reported perceptions of business people and country analysts. A country with the rank of 1 has the least corruption.

[51] The Economist Intelligence Unit (EIU), *Country Report: South Africa,* September 2008.

[52] "South Africa Leader Welcomes G20" BBC, April 3, 2009.

[53] EIU, "South Africa: Power Down," January 31, 2008.

[54] "South African Power Cuts Threaten Economic Growth; Jobs," *VOA News*, January 31, 2008.

[55] For more information see CRS Report RL32773, *The Global Peace Operations Initiative: Background and Issues for Congress*, by Nina M. Serafino.

[56] On December 26, the President signed into law the FY2008 Consolidated Appropriations Act (H.R. 2764/P.L. 110- 16 1), which included State, Foreign Operations, and Related Programs appropria-

tions for FY2008. Country-specific allocations have not yet been released.
[57] "Congressman Wants to End U.S. Travel Restrictions against Mandela and the ANC," *Voice of America*, April 10, 2008.
[58] "SA, US Work in Tandem to Find Terrorist Cells," *Business Day*, December 11, 2002.
[59] "Spreading Influence: In South Africa, Mounting Evidence of al Qaeda Links," *Wall Street Journal*, December 10, 2002.
[60] "Arrests and Plots Give South Africans a New Program," *New York Times,* August 9, 2004.
[61] U.S. Department of State, 2005 Country Reports on Terrorism http://www.state.gov/s/ct/rls/crt/2005/.
[62] "Law Enforcement," available at the website of the U.S. Embassy in Pretoria http://usembassy.state.gov/pretoria.
[63] Janine Zacharia, "U.S. Finds an Antagonist in a Country on the Rise," *International Herald Tribune*, June 27, 2007.
[64] Remarks by Deputy Assistant Secretary of State Linda Thomas-Greenfield, "U.S.-South Africa Relations: The View from Washington," Washington, D.C., September 14, 2006.
[65] According to South African media reports, in July 2007, the U.S. Ambassador to South Africa, Eric Bost, publicly expressed frustration that the country's defense minister would not respond to requests for a meeting with General Kip Ward, commander of AFRICOM. For more information, see CRS Report RL34003, *Africa Command: U.S. Strategic Interests and the Role of the U.S. Military in Africa*, by Lauren Ploch.
[66] "South Africa's Support for Iran's Nuclear Program 'Holds Firm'," *BBC Monitoring Africa*, September 1, 2006.
[67] See, for example, Colum Lynch, "South Africa's U.N. Votes Disappoint Some," *Washington Post*, April 16, 2007; James Kirchick, "Why, the Beloved Country?," *Los Angeles Times*, July 29, 2007.
[68] U.N. document, S/2007/14, January 12, 2007.
[69] "Britain Wants U.N. Security Council Attention on Zimbabwe," *Voice of America*, March 16, 2007.
[70] "Desmond Tutu 'deeply disappointed with South Africa's vote against U.N Security Council resolution on Myanmar,"*International Herald Tribune*, January 21, 2007.
[71] "South Africa Reportedly Blocking U.N. Debate on Zimbabwe Crisis," *Business Day*, March 20, 2007.

[72] China, Indonesia, the Russian Federation, and Qatar also abstained. U.N. document, S/2007/3 15, May 30, 2007.

[73] U.N. Document S/Res/1747, March 24, 2007. For South African government statements on the vote, see "Iran Keeps Up Nuclear Consultation with SA," *Business Day,* July 9, 2007.

[74] For more information on South Africa's policies on Zimbabwe, see CRS Report RL34509, *Zimbabwe: The Power Sharing Agreement and Implications for U.S. Policy*, by Lauren Ploch.

[75] Comments made by President Bush during press conference on July 9, 2003 in Pretoria http://www.whitehouse.gov/ news/releases/2003/07/ 20030709.html.

[76] "Zimbabwe Pays Part of IMF Debt," *The Washington Post,* September 2, 2005.

[77] "The Real Fraud in Zimbabwe," *The Washington Times*, April 6, 2005.

[78] "Zimbabwe's Enabler; South Africa Falls Short as Monitor of Democracy, *The Washington Post*, April 4, 2005.

[79] "We Are Not Quiet Diplomats," *Daily Mail and Guardian* (Johannesburg), November 5, 2004.

[80] "South Africa Ends 's 'Silence' on Zimbabwe, Urges Harare 'to Respect Rule of Law,'" *BBC Monitoring Africa*, March 14, 2007.

[81] "I'm No Mugabe, but I Have Sympathy for What He Has Done," *The Sunday Telegraph* (London), November 26, 2006.

[82] "Chorus of Disapproval Grows As Sexwale Speaks Out on Mugabe," *Zimbabwe Independent*, October 6, 2006.

[83] "Zimbabwe 'Ignoring' SA Diplomacy," *BBC*, May 15, 2007.

[84] Barry Bearak, "Zimbabwe Opponent Criticizes Mbeki," *New York Times*, February 14, 2008.

[85] Michael Gerson, "The Despots' Democracy," *Washington Post*, May 28, 2008.

[86] "Anxiety Grows for Kidnaped Zimbabwe Activist," Voice of America, May 18, 2008.

[87] U.S. International Trade Commission.

[88] For further information, see CRS Report RS21387, *United States-Southern African Customs Union (SACU) Free Trade Agreement Negotiations: Background and Potential Issues*, by Danielle Langton.

[89] See, for example, President Mbeki's December 16, 2002 address to the ANC national conference http://www.anc.org.za/ancdocs/history/ mbeki/2002/tm1216.html.

In: U.S. Political and Trade Relations with Africa ISBN 978-1-61209-956-9
Editor: Gregory D. Ferro © 2012 Nova Science Publishers, Inc.

Chapter 4

GHANA: BACKGROUND AND U.S. RELATIONS*

Nicolas Cook

ABSTRACT

This report provides information on current developments in Ghana and Ghana's relations with the United States, which are close. It describes the purpose of President Barack Obama's forthcoming trip to Ghana, which will focus on issues of good governance and socio-economic and political development, and characterizes the current state of play in bilateral relations. It also summarizes the policy agenda of Ghana's president, John Atta Mills, who won office by a narrow margin in elections in late 2008. The dynamics of that election are described in the report, as are recent policy-centered developments, economic challenges and performance, and socio-economic prospects. Ghana's international relations and bilateral development cooperation with the United States are also covered in the report.

* This is an edited, reformatted and augmented version of CRS Report RS22809, dated July 8, 2009.

Overview and Current Developments

President Barack Obama is slated to travel to Ghana from July 10 to 11, following the president's attendance at the G-8 Summit in L'Aquila, Italy. Key purposes of the trip, discussed further below, are to highlight Ghana as "a shining example" in Africa "of the importance of free and fair elections"; to underscore "the critical role that sound governance and civil society play in promoting lasting development" in Africa; and to stress the continuing commitment of the United States to invest in such development [1].

The trip will also provide a forum for discussions between President Obama and President John Atta Mills of Ghana, one of the United States' "most trusted partners in sub-Saharan Africa" on "a range of bilateral and regional issues" [2].

President Obama's trip to Ghana comes almost exactly six months after the inauguration of President Mills, following presidential and parliamentary elections in December 2008. President Obama had previously characterized these elections, which at the presidential level were reportedly among the closest ever in post-colonial Africa, as demonstrating "the Ghanaian people's commitment to democratic governance" and as an exemplar of Ghana's "democratic leadership in Africa, particularly in light of the troubling coups in Mauritania, Guinea, and Madagascar." [3]. The 2008 election marked Ghana's fifth consecutive democratic national election and preceded its second democratic transfer of power from one political party to another. This watershed, a rare occurrence in post-independence sub-Saharan Africa, signified Ghana's further maturation as a democracy following a transition from "no-party" rule that began in 1992.

U.S.-Ghanaian relations are warm. President Obama's trip follows an early 2008 trip by former President George W. Bush to Ghana, which in 2006 signed a $547 million U.S. Millennium Challenge Corporation (MCC) Compact. The goal of President Bush's 2008 trip, during which he also visited several other African countries, was to personally review MCC and other U.S. aid programs in Africa. He held talks with former Ghanaian President John Agyekum Kufuor and other African leaders on prospective continued U.S.-African partnership to sustain "democratic reform, respect for human rights, free trade, open investment regimes, and economic opportunity" across Africa. His visit to Ghana focused on improved health prospects for Ghana resulting from its designation in 2008 as a President's Malaria Initiative focus country; prospective education improvements resulting from Ghana's participation in the President's Expanded Education Initiative; and trade growth efforts under the U.S. African Global Competitiveness Initiative (AGCI). The AGCI West Africa Trade Hub, which promotes intra-African and U.S.-African trade, is based in Ghana, which also hosts the U.S. Agency for International Development (USAID) regional development program.

Apart from development cooperation, Ghana is widely seen as a key U.S. partner in the region and as an African "success story" in light of its successful transition to democracy and attainment of substantial economic gains in recent years, albeit in the face of continuing widespread poverty rates. It is a stable country in an often volatile sub-region, and has helped to mediate several political and/or military conflicts in West Africa over the last quarter century. It is also praised for its near-constant contribution of troops to international peacekeeping operations in Africa and elsewhere. Ghana has also drawn attention recently because of its recent discovery of a sizable reserve of crude oil. This reserve promises to boost national income and development prospects, but—based on the experience of many other oil-rich developing countries—may also pose substantial good governance and resource management challenges. Ghana, like the United States, also faces challenges with respect to narcotics trafficking, notably with respect to a rise in recent years of cocaine being transported from South America to Europe via West Africa, and a shared interest in countering such trafficking is a growing area of U.S.-Ghanaian cooperation [4].

President Obama's Trip to Ghana

President Obama's trip to Ghana is being preceded by a multi-leg trip to other countries, including a visit to Russia for bilateral talks and to Italy and the Vatican for bilateral meetings, the G8 summit and related meetings [5]. The latter are substantially to focus on African and developing country issues. They include a "G8-plus-5-plus-1" meeting (i.e., a meeting of the G8 plus five major emerging economies, China, India, South Africa, Mexico, and Brazil, plus Egypt, which was invited to participate by Italy) and a working breakfast of the G8 plus African countries and five international organizations, as well as a U.S. bilateral meeting with South Africa, among other meetings.

According to presidential African affairs aide Michelle Gavin, President Obama's trip to Ghana is meant to signal his particular interest "in emphasizing themes of governance—the importance of governance for making development progress [and...] for stability" in Africa and the broader developing world. Ghana was chosen, she said, because "Ghana is a truly admirable example of a place where governance is getting stronger, a thriving democracy," a status exemplified by the election of 2008. The election was laudable, she suggested, because despite the narrow margin between the two run-off contestants, and in contrast to many political crisis-generating elections in multiple other African countries, in Ghana "power was transferred peacefully" to a new government that "continue[s] to pursue a development agenda and bolster the rule of law." [6].

Gavin stated that while in Ghana, President Obama would have discussions with President Mills "about a number of important issues" in furtherance of what she characterized as a "strong bilateral relationship." Issues to be discussed include "development priorities, including agricultural development" and "governance issues," the latter contextualized in Ghana's anticipated "challenges as a new oil wealth is slated to come online within the next couple years" which, she said, "always creates an interesting governance challenge." Other issues slated to be addressed, Gavin said, include food security, maternal health and mortality, and "regional issues... relating to stability, governance, counternarcotics, which is an important issue in West Africa"—all issues of current interest within the 111th Congress [7].

The President is also slated to give a speech about some of the themes that are being addressed in his discussions with President Mills. The speech is the last of a four-part thematic series of overseas speeches laying out some of President Obama's key foreign policy views, and is to center on the relationship between democracy and development in Africa and in the wider developing world [8]. It is slated, in particular, to focus on the importance of good governance and the need to institutionalize of an interplay between elected officials, voters, civil society and local initiatives in achieving that end. The speech is also expected to focus on the key role played by national self determination and achievement in attaining socio-economic and political development, in contrast to donor-led development. Following the speech, President Obama and Mrs. Obama are slated to visit to Cape Coast, along Ghana's central coast, which is the location of the Cape Coast Slave Castle, a key holding point for slaves prior to their forced trans-Atlantic passage to the Americas.

In contextualizing the Africa portion of President Obama's trip in relation to his preceding visit to Russia and Italy, Ms. Gavin characterized the Ghana visit as "quite intentional" and meant to underscore "the point that Africa is integrated broadly into" the Administration's foreign policy strategy and that "African voices are an important part of global discussions on key global issues." She and other briefers highlighted the fact that African governments would participate in a number of meetings at the G8 summit. Gavin also drew a correlation between the issue themes being discussed at the G8 summit and policy challenges faced by African countries, such as a need for economic resilience, a capacity to weather the current economic downturn, achieve socio-economic development goals, as well as global issues, such as climate change—and what she characterized as the underlying importance of good governance in successfully addressing them.

Mills Administration

President Mills took office on January 7, 2009, succeeding former President Kufuor after the latter's second term in office. The new government's first priority reportedly centered on gaining control over economic policy administration and the government's administrative apparatus from the departing NPP government. In particular, it reportedly sought to stabilize the declining exchange rate of the national currency, the cedi; halt a rapid rise in fiscal spending, leading to a rising current account deficit; and check inflation. These challenges have been compounded by the global recession, a strengthening dollar, a slowing economy, due in part to weakening commodity prices and a contraction of access to international and local credit, but have been aided by a decline in imports and growth in exports [9].

Policy Agenda

Mills, as stated in his 2009 state of the nation address to parliament, has pledged to fulfill the goals outlined in the NDC party election platform [10]. Key policy areas addressed under the manifesto include governance; economic growth and investment; investment in people (e.g., health sector and education); and investments in infrastructure for growth [11].

Governance

The Mills government has pledged to undertake a number of administrative reforms to prevent government corruption and strengthen the organizations that investigate and prosecute corruption, including by insulating the Serious Fraud Office from political interference, and by passing a Freedom of Information Bill to ensure public access to official information. It also proposes substantial capacity building of computer-based systems to enforce efficient and transparent use of public funds and bolster administrative oversight of government activities.

Profile: President John Mills

Ghana's current president, Dr. John Evans Fiifi Mills, popularly known as the "The Prof," was born in July 1944 at Tarkwa in Ghana's Western Region. Prior to being elected in 2008, he had twice—in 2000 and in 2004— unsuccessfully competed for the presidency as the candidate of the National Democratic Congress (NDC) against former President Kufuor of the New Patriotic Party (NPP). Mills had previously served as Ghana's national Vice President from 1997 to 2001 in the administration of former president Jerry Rawlings. A former national tax commissioner and professor of law at the University of Ghana, Legon, Mills holds a BA in law from the University of Ghana, Legon and a PhD in Law from the School of Oriental and African Studies in London, the United Kingdom, where he wrote a dissertation focusing on taxation and economic development. He also attended Stanford Law School as a Fulbright scholar and has taught and lectured at several foreign institution of higher learning. He has served as a board or executive member or examiner at multiple high-level Ghanaian national financial, economic, and business institutions. President Mills is married to Ernestina Naadu Mills, an educator, and has a son, Sam Kofi Mills. The relationship between Mills and Rawlings is a delicate one for Mills. Rawlings, the founder of the NDC, is a charismatic former president who, despite having no reported further aspirations for public office, is viewed as maintaining a popular base of support within the NDC. He regularly comments on current events and national political personalities, often in a no-holds barred manner that often provokes controversy. He is viewed as having brought Mills to national political prominence by selecting Mills as his vice presidential NDC party running mate in the 1996 election. There has long been speculation in the Ghanaian press over whether Rawlings wields influence over Mills, who once provoked controversy by stating that he would consult with Rawlings if elected. While there is some concordance between some policy actions advocated by Rawlings and those taken by Mills, it is not clear that these reflect Rawlings's influence, and not simply shared policy views. There are also some signs of differences between the two men. Rawlings has criticized Mills's selection of nominees for government leadership posts, and accused him of failing to more forcefully push for probes or prosecution of allegedly corrupt Kufuor Administration figures. In addition, while some former Rawlings administration officials occupy posts in the Mills Administration, Mills has reportedly sidelines other Rawlings associates, suggesting that Mills is his own man.

Sources: NDC, "The Candidate," n.d., http://www.attamills2008.com ; Ghana Review International, "Professor John Evans Mills (NDC)," n.d., http://www.ghanareview.com; Africa Confidential, "Is Rawlings the back-seat driver?," February 6, 2009 and "The Mills grind slowly," April 17, 2009; and BBC News, "Profile: Ghana President John Mills," January 3, 2009.

It also seeks to ensure increased and equitable access to justice, through judicial system capacity-building, the use of alternative dispute resolution mechanisms and legal aid, and efforts to prevent the corrupt or political manipulation of justice. The NDC has also promised increased national and public security through diverse efforts to build national border control, police, intelligence, and military capacities and personnel diversity, and resolve several political murders.

The government is, in particular, seeking to bring such assets to bear on counternarcotics activities. The manifesto states that Mills's NDC government will seek to "reverse Ghana's image as an easy target for money laundering and [illicit] drug transport" through asset seizures, correlate drug prosecution assets and the severity of resulting sentences with the "seriousness of the crime," including by targeting high-level drug criminals and "their powerful allies." The Mills Administration also seeks to increase the role of women in government decision and policy-making by increasing to "at least 40%" the representation of women in government, public service and in the NDC; increase the role of women in education; make "reproductive and other female health issues central" to social and health policy; and promote education and legislative measures to ensure women's rights. It also seeks to increase representative and decentralized governance and accountability at the local level through various means; enhance operational proficiency, profitability, and the accountability of public sector companies.

Economic Growth

The NDC manifesto calls for pursuit of an "activist and enabling state" that will help boost business growth and credit access, notably to small businesses, many part of the large informal sector, including through the provision of tax breaks to financial institutions that help achieve these goals. It also calls for the government to facilitate "fair" and legal access to land and property ownership titles; enact business-friendly regulatory reform; and boost job creation, especially for Ghana's youthful population. It also seeks to promote Ghana's access to international markets by pursuing efforts to gain "relief in international trade arrangements to protect domestic industry"; increase export promotion efforts; providing aid to Economic Community of West African States (ECOWAS) countries "in exchange for export markets for Ghanaian made goods"; and by privileging public procurement purchases of Ghanaian goods.

The document also calls for efforts to make Ghana a financial hub for finance in West Africa, build the local banking sector, and enhance bank regulation by the Bank of Ghana. It also lays out a local industrial support policy focused particularly on decentralization of industrialization, duty- free treatment for industries targeted for high-priority growth. These include agriculture processing, textiles, mining, petro-chemicals, fertilizer, salt, and cement production, pharmaceuticals, afro-forestry and wood products, shea, housing and road construction. Agricultural growth is a particular target of the government's economic growth policy, and the manifesto lays out a wide range of efforts to aid the farm sector, ranging from diverse production growth and technology enhancing strategies to increased access to credit and markets to diverse types of agricultural infrastructure growth. The key cocoa industry, as well as the cotton, cashew, rubber, oil palm, soy, fruit, shea nut, timber, and coconut crop sectors, along with bio-fuel and medicinal plants and fisheries, are especially targeted to receive such assistance. Mining reforms, particularly in support of local mining communities, are another focal policy area for the government.

Social and Infrastructure Investment

Key foci of the social investment to investment policies of the Mills Administration, as outlined in the NDC manifesto, include health Care-related efforts to address "malnutrition, poor sanitation, unsafe water, poverty and a shortage of health care providers' equal high infant and maternal mortality, [and] large gaps in health care between urban and rural, rich and poor." The means for achieving such ends include expanding access to quality, affordable basic primary health services through diverse administrative reforms, greater medical personnel training and compensation.

Increased access to education is another key policy goal, and efforts in this area center on increasing teacher training, motivation, and retention and expanding access to free primary; technical and vocational education; and tertiary education.

The government also supports a wide range of programs to alleviate poverty, ranging from adult illiteracy efforts to increased transparency in government development efforts to increased access to water, sanitation and social services. Urban slum renovation and increased access to housing and jobs by the poor in cities is another major element of poverty alleviation efforts by the government, but it also seeks to decrease rural poverty, primarily by boosting agriculture and access to infrastructure and transportation.

Infrastructure growth is the final major policy priority of the Mills Administration. According to the NDC manifesto, the government will seek to expand housing, access to water and sanitation, and transport infrastructure through a mix of regulatory reforms, technical efficiency advancements, and basic construction investments.

Electricity sector reforms and investment and transparent effective governance and use of what is expected to be a very large influx of oil revenues in future years are among the other major policy elements of the Administration's policy agenda.

2008 Election

Ghana held presidential and parliamentary elections on December 7, 2008, resulting in a marginal electoral win for the NDC. The election campaign was contested vigorously but was reportedly largely peaceful. Focal electoral issues included public dissatisfaction over electricity and water shortages, rising food, fuel, and utility prices, and reports of corruption [12]. Recent economic expansion and prospective oil revenue-fueled growth, however, were seen as benefitting the NPP, as were divisions in the NDC, from which a dissenting faction broke away to form a new splinter party. While Mills was selected as the NDC presidential candidate, notwithstanding his two earlier losses as NDC flag bearer, 18 NPP candidates fiercely vied for the NPP nomination in the run-up to the NPP party congress in late 2007. Akufo-Addo won the nomination in the first round of voting, surprising some observers, given that President Kufuor had reportedly favored another candidate. The NPP nomination process drew some criticism because the $25,000 party nomination fee, in a country with an average income of about $520, was seen as barring contenders who lacked wealth or could not raise large amounts of cash to rally support [13]. Ghana generally enjoys inter-ethnic harmony, but regional rivalries and disparities that are sometimes viewed in ethnic terms play a role in politics [14]. Ethnicity, however, does not appear to have played an overt or key role in the election.

With some minor, mostly technical exceptions, voting on December 7 was free, open, and transparent, according to reports by national and international observers who monitored the vote, along with a large number of national political party observers [15]. The election elicited widespread praise internationally, despite some minor shortcomings [16]. These reportedly included temporary shortages of voting materials at some polling places, along with limited, minor allegations of irregularities, mainly in two constituencies, Asutifi South and Akwatia [17]. In the initial presidential vote, John Mills of the opposition National Democratic Congress (NDC) party won a 47.92% vote share. His main rival, former Foreign Affairs Minister Nana Addo Dankwa Akufo-Addo of the New Patriotic Party (NPP)—President Kufuor's party and the majority party after the previous election in 2004—won a 49.13% vote share. Given that neither leading candidate attained a 50% vote share, a requirement for electoral victory, a run-off vote was later held. In the December 7 parliamentary vote, the opposition NDC achieved a narrow majority, winning 114 (5 0%) of 228 seats for which results had been determined as of January 6, 2009—of a total of 230 seats—against 107 (nearly 47%) seats for the NPP. Seven additional seats were won by two minor parties and independent candidates. The winners of two seats had not been certified as of January 6, 2009.

A presidential run-off vote between Mills and Akufo-Addo was held in 229 constituencies on December 28, resulting in a 50.13% vote share for Mills, with Akufo-Addo winning 49.87% of the vote, 23,050 votes fewer than Mills [18]. These results failed to decide the election, however, because incorrect allocations of voting materials were delivered to one constituency, Tain District, in the central Brong Ahafo Region, potentially disenfranchising voters [19]. This discrepancy prompted the Electoral Commission to order a repeat of runoff balloting in Tain, an outcome that conferred on Tain's estimated 53,000 voters the potential power to decide the outcome of the race [20]. Although the NPP considered a legal challenge to and later a political boycott of the Tain vote, which was controversial and spurred some very minor, isolated post-election violence, it later accepted the outcome [21]. After Tain was added to the national run-off totals, Mills garnered a winning 50.23% share of votes cast against a 49.77% vote share for Akufo-Addo [22].

Kufuor Record

Kufuor, a former veteran opposition figure and Oxford-trained lawyer, businessman, and former deputy foreign minister and parliamentarian, was ineligible to run for the presidency in 2008 due to constitutional term limits. He first won the presidency in 2000, having bested Mills in a poll that led to Ghana's widely praised, first-ever democratic presidential and political party succession. In 2004, he again triumphed over Mills, winning 52% of votes in a poll that was generally calm, peaceful, and transparent, though marred by limited violence [23]. In simultaneous parliamentary elections, Kufuor 's New Patriotic Party (NPP) increased its legislative margin by 26%, winning 128 seats, while the NDC won 94. Two smaller parties and an independent won all other seats [24]. Kufuor used the slogan "So far, so good" to claim a solid record of economic stability, market-based reforms and growth, and broad quality of life improvements after a period of economic stagnation under the NDC.

Kufuor's reelection in 2004 marked Ghana's fourth consecutive democratic election. Ghana appeared to have durably consolidated a transition to democratic rule that began in 1992, when the then-military leader, Jerry Rawlings, retired from the military to run as a civilian presidential candidate in multiparty elections. Rawlings had first come to power in a 1979 military coup, after which elections were held. He led a second military coup in 1981, establishing a populist, reform- oriented ruling civil-military entity, the Provisional National Defense Council (PNDC). The PNDC coup followed 15 years of coups d'état and a string of military-dominated, often corrupt governments that ruled after the military ousted Kwame Nkrumah, Ghana's first elected Prime Minister, in 1966. He was toppled shortly after he transformed Ghana into a one-party state. Nkrumah, famous advocate of African unity and socialism, led Ghana to independence from Britain in 1957. Ghana celebrated its 50th year of independence in 2007.

Kufuor 's first-term agenda emphasized efforts to bolster national unity and social equity after the 2000 election; to fight reportedly widespread corruption; to reassert the rule of law; and to revive a flagging economy. Upon taking office, he faced diverse poor economic indicators: flat growth; currency deflation; poor or declining prices for key commodity exports (gold and cocoa); high inflation, interest, and unemployment; and dependence on foreign aid. Kufuor vowed to tackle these problems aggressively, but faced a roughly evenly party-divided legislature and a NDCdominated bureaucracy. He met these challenges by taking steps to privatize state firms, diversify the economy, increase Ghana's world market access, and pursue politically difficult fiscal austerity policies. Ghana continues to face multiple economic challenges, but the Kufuor administration has achieved many of its initial goals, including substantial utility deregulation, an increase in hard currency reserves, and high economic growth rates.

ECONOMY

Ghana's export earnings have grown in recent years; they stood at about $5.2 billion in 2008, are estimated at $5.7 billion in 2009, and are projected to rise to $5.9 billion in 2010 [25]. In June 2007, the discovery of offshore light crude oil reserves conservatively estimated in the 450-550 million barrel range, has boosted future export earning prospects. The economy grew at an estimated annual rate of 7.3% in 2008 but fell to 4.7% in 2009, according to the Economist Intelligence Unit, which forecasts a slightly higher rate of growth of 5.4% in 2010. Inflation, which had been around 10% in 2008, low by historical standards, rose to an estimated 16.8% in 2009, but is expected to decline to around 11% in 2010 [26]. Domestic savings rates are rising, and a large influx of expatriate remittances has boosted growth, notably in construction. The small Ghana Stock Exchange has boomed in recent years, and in 2003 Ghana received its first sovereign credit rating, which has since been upgraded. In September 2007, it successfully and for the first time raised $750 million in international Eurobond issues. Ghana largely successfully fulfilled its World Bank and International Monetary Fund (IMF)-backed Ghana Poverty Reduction Strategy (GPRS). In part due to this, Ghana has received debt relief under the Heavily Indebted Poor Countries Initiative and the Multilateral Debt Relief Initiative. This is leading to additional international financial institution assistance, and has resulted in a series of actual or planned debt write-offs by bilateral creditors totaling about $3.5 billion. The World Bank's 2006/07 Doing Business report ranked Ghana third among 10 global "Top Reformers" based on gains in public service provision, contract mediation, import operations, and reductions in red tape for property and business start-ups.

Social indicators have steadily improved. Ghana reportedly may become the first African country to surpass the United Nations Millennium Development Goal of halving poverty by 2015. Rising commodity prices, notably of key exports like cocoa and gold, as well as growth in tourism, have played a major role in economic growth. The Kufuor administration also attributed Ghana's recent economic successes to fiscal discipline, improved revenue collection, and to the government's policy agenda. It emphasized liberal, private sector-focused economic reform goals and efforts to promote good governance and improve living standards.

The Kufuor government also reportedly boosted investment in education, healthcare delivery, communications, and infrastructure. The latter is fairly developed by regional standards but in many cases is aging or inadequate to meet future demands. The Kufuor government also sought to address possible socio-economic and regulatory challenges arising from a forecast rise in oil earnings. The Kufuor Administration established a state task force to study ways to ensure that such funds are used for socially equitable economic diversification projects and to develop the nascent oil sector.

The Kufuor Administration also planned to create a national stabilization fund to minimize economic growth shocks and revenue volatility associated with its dependence on cocoa, gold, timber and oil exports. Oil management and transparency issues and policy challenges are discussed in detail in a recent report by Oxfam America and the Integrated Social Development Center (ISODEC), a Ghanaian policy institute [27].

Economic and Related Policy Prospects

Despite much economic success, poverty remains widespread, notably among the rural majority. From 1997-2003, 40% of Ghanaians lived below the poverty line. Joblessness also remains high. Poverty rates are slowly declining, however, and the average annual income of $590 in 2007 has grown markedly from the 2003 level of $300. The economy remains highly rural and agricultural, even though about 47% of the population is urban, which is high by regional standards. Agriculture employs about 60% of workers, and contributes about 37% of annual gross domestic product (GDP). Services, notably the information technology and financial sectors, have expanded rapidly and are eclipsing agriculture; they contribute an estimated 3 7-40% of GDP.

Ghana has established a small offshore call and information processing industry, and several new banks have been created. Industry, notably the gold mining sector, has also grown substantially; it provides nearly 25% of annual GDP. The government supports the extensive small-scale and informal sectors through the use of micro-loans and small business-friendly policies. A key challenge is an insufficient electricity supply. The Kufuor government pursued several national and international regional power generation or distribution projects and efforts to liberalize the electricity sector. One regional effort, the U.S.-backed West African Gas Pipeline, which is slated to bring natural gas from Nigeria to Ghana and it eastern neighbors, had faced repeated delays, but came online in mid-December 2007 [28]. Other key economic challenges include low wages and productivity rates, and high oil and food prices. Floods in 2007 also devastated northern towns and farms.

Transparency and accountability were key goals of the Kufuor administration, as they are for that of President Mills. The Kufuor administration backed passage of several anti-corruption and public sector transparency laws, made Ghana a participant in the Extractive Industries Transparency Initiative (EITI, an international revenue transparency effort), and signed and ratified the African Union convention on corruption, among other actions. Corruption, nevertheless, has remained a problem. Public sector bribery is reportedly common, and there have been several high profile corruption cases involving top officials. Some critics contend that anti-corruption law enforcement is often weak. Notwithstanding the Kufuor government's private sector orientation and diverse achievements, the State Department's FY2008 Congressional Budget Justification, mirroring the views of some other observers, stated that Ghana "remains a difficult place to do business; contract sanctity, clear land title, and expeditious licensing regimes present daunting challenges. Schools are inadequate, and quality health care is unavailable for many, particularly, for the poor and the disenfranchised."

International Relations

Ghana's government has actively mediated in crises in Liberia, Cote d'Ivoire, and Togo. Some observers believe that its close relations with the late Gnassingbe Eyadema, former president of Togo, may have caused it to take a moderate stance vis-à-vis Togo's 2005 leadership succession and electoral crisis, which led about 12,000 Togolese to enter Ghana as refugees. Some human rights advocates also criticized Ghana's decision to facilitate the return of Charles Taylor, former president of Liberia, to his country from peace talks in 2003 in Ghana after he was indicted for war crimes by the U.S.-backed Special Court for Sierra Leone [29]. Ghana contributes a considerable number of troops to international peacekeeping operations, notably within Africa. It is seen as having an increasingly professional military, following decades of military intervention in state politics. Ghana is also active in helping to develop African peacekeeping capacities; it hosts a regional peacekeeping training center. The United States has provided training and equipment to the center. Ghana was elected to chair the African Union in 2007 and hosted the 9th African Union Summit in July 2007. It also served as a U.N. Security Council member, 2006-2007. Like many African countries, Ghana is pursuing greater economic cooperation and trade ties with China, and has increased its exports to China, notably manganese and cocoa.

U.S. RELATIONS

U.S.-Ghanaian relations are close — as discussed in the Overview and Current Developments of this report — and a small population of Americans, many of African-American descent, has settled permanently in Ghana. The Obama Administration regards Ghana as "a stable and democratic country" and as among the "most trusted partners" of the United States in Africa," a sentiment that reflects broad continuity with the Bush Administration's view of Ghana [30]. In part, this strong partnership is due to the Obama Administration's view of Ghana's status as "a leader in promoting peaceful conflict resolution in Africa" and as a major troop contributor to international peacekeeping missions [31]. Ghana is a leading African buyer of U.S. goods, but bilateral trade, while growing, is relatively small. In 2008, U.S. exports to Ghana totaled $609million, up from $416 million in 2007 and a $314 million average in 2005 and 2006. U.S. imports from Ghana stood at $222 million in 2008, up from $199 million in 2007 and an average of $175 million in 2005 and 2006. They have grown steadily, from $115 million in 2002. Ghana is eligible for all trade benefits under the U.S. African Growth and Opportunity Act (AGOA) and in mid-2007 hosted the 6th AGOA Forum.

Bilateral Assistance

While the Obama Administration views Ghana positively, it also sees it as facing a number of substantial development and other challenges. According to the State Department's FY2010 *Congressional Budget Justification for Foreign Operations*, Ghana

> faces numerous challenges, including weak institutions, over-centralization of authority, corruption, and a growing narcotics trafficking problem. In addition, the Ghanaian health system is struggling, while Ghanaians suffer from a heavy burden of disease, especially malaria. In the past decade, there has been no improvement in maternal and infant morality rates. HIV infects almost 20,000 people each year. Access to education has improved, but quality remains poor and only about a quarter of primary school students can read at grade level.

U.S. assistance is targeted at helping Ghana to address these challenges [32].

Governance

Recent U.S. Agency for International Development (USAID)-administered democratization assistance to Ghana has supported decentralization efforts and greater citizen participation in governance, notably at the local and regional level; improved parliamentary law-making and oversight skills; better local government service capacity; and efforts to build civil society capacities to influence government policy making. It has also supported anti-corruption reform, in particular efforts to strengthen public official assets declaration requirements, bolster public support for the creation of public official conflict of interest guidelines, and to expand information sharing among accountability institutions [33].

U.S. assistance helped ensure that the 2008 election was transparent and successful. A USAIDfunded project implemented by the National Democratic Institute in partnership with the Ghana Center for Democratic Development (CDD) helped train election observers prior to the 2008 elections. The resulting Coalition of Domestic Election Observers (CODEO) played a key role in ensuring transparency and public confidence in the 2008 pre-election and election polling processes [34]. CODEO issued a series of assessments of the pre-election environment, conditions during polling, and carried out a statistically significant parallel sample vote tabulation based on actual polling data that very accurately predicted the election outcome and helped to assure the public that the polling results were legitimate and accurate [35].

U.S. assistance planned by the Obama Administration in FY 2010 calls for USAID to provide direct technical assistance to continue fiscal decentralization and strengthening of local government skills to enable them to more effectively and transparently plan, budget, implement, and monitor programs. In addition it is to support local development-focused engagement between local government entities and citizen advocacy groups regarding local priorities and strategies for achieving them. U.S. assistance is also slated to support governance and institutional capacity building pertaining to such policy and program areas as health, education, water access, and economic growth. In part, this aid is aimed at bolstering the general ability of state institutions to effectively and responsibly manage public resources prior to the anticipated large increases in oil revenues in coming years.

Investing in People

Recent U.S. USAID-administered health sector assistance to Ghana focuses on preventing HIV/AIDS, malaria, and tuberculosis; increasing health services delivery, particularly focused on maternal health and child survival and malnutrition; and improving state healthcare planning, management, and accountability capabilities. Ghana became a President's Malaria Initiative (PMI) country in FY2008. The Obama Administration's FY2010 CBJ assistance plan for Ghana calls for continued USAID support in these areas, particularly with respect to preventive and other health services, including increased access to voluntary family planning methods, at the community and district-level; a Ghana Ministry of Health plan to promote results-based management and performance-based financing in the health sector.

It also calls for infrastructure development, behavior change communication related to water and sanitation access and use, and development of local government and civil society organizations to manage such infrastructure. PMI assistance is slated to focus on scaling up "proven preventive and treatment interventions to achieve of 85% coverage among vulnerable groups in order to reach the PMI goal of reducing malaria-related morbidity by 50%," particularly centering on increasing access to insecticide-treated bed-nets. The Obama Administration also plans to provide Ghana with substantial support under the President's Emergency Plan for AIDS Relief (PEPFAR) focused on strengthening integrated HIV/AIDS prevention, care and treatment programs across Ghana and supporting orphans and vulnerable children. U.S. Basic Education assistance is slated to support efforts to improve early grade competencies, e.g. "literacy, numeracy, arithmetic, and basic personal finance, basic scientific concepts, general health, including awareness of malaria and HIV/AIDS." U.S. assistance will also focus on improving teacher training, "dramatically increasing" access to learning materials, and monitoring and evaluating progress of the programs using empirical and quantifiable metrics.

Economic Growth

Recent USAID Development Assistance program activity has focused on boosting agricultural marketing and export potential, small business capacity building, and market liberalization reforms. It has also supported policy reforms aimed at supporting macro-economic stability, liberalizing agricultural input markets, and supporting policy-making capacities related to finance, labor and land regulation, energy, natural resource management, and information and communication technology. FY2010 Development Assistance planned by the Obama Administration is intended to continue to support many of these objectives, but will in particular focus on objectives set out in various Ghanaian government sectoral plans and programs (e.g., those focusing on trade, the financial sector, and the food and agricultural sectors).

In particular, U.S. assistance will seek to strengthen Ghanaian government policy-making aimed at boosting private sector performance and will also help small-and medium-sized agricultural businesses meet regulatory and market-based standards and attract foreign investors. USAID is also designing a new Agriculture Trade and Investment program intended to scale up prior USAID programs to help increase commercial relations between producer organizations and buyers and expand assistance targeting small-holder farmers, particularly with respect to high- value horticulture crops. U.S. assistance will also help Ghana to achieve food security by boosting market-based production, processing, transport and marketing and trade of staple foods, e.g., maize, cassava and soybeans, and improving the balance between food supplies and demands within the entire sub-regional of which Ghana is a part. In part, this end will be pursued through diverse competitiveness, credit access, transport, trade capacity building programs and business policy reforms under the U.S. Global Food Security Response (GFSR) program. GFSR seeks to rapidly improve access to and production and distribution of staple foods.36 Ghanaians also benefit from trade and export-related technical assistance under the regional USAID African Global Competitiveness Initiative (AGCI). A sub-regional AGCI Trade Hub is located in Ghana. It provides trade, investment, and business information and technical assistance to African and U.S. public and private sector business, trade, and policy entities [37].

Peace, Security, and Counternarcotics

Limited Foreign Military Financing, International Narcotics Control and Law Enforcement, and Nonproliferation, Antiterrorism, and Demining and Related Project funds support peace and security and law enforcement capacity-building [38]. Military and police assistance centers on helping Ghana to counter its growing use as a key cocaine transshipment point in the region, in large part by increasing its ability to control its borders and key entry and trade points, in part to ensure that "Ghana does not serve as a base or transit point for illicit shipments of people, goods, and narcotics to the United States."

In addition to capacity building assistance administered by the State Department's Bureau of International Narcotics and Law Enforcement Affairs (INL), U.S. counternarcotics assistance to Ghana is being pursued by the Drug Enforcement Administration (DEA). DEA recently set up a country office in Ghana, and is in the process of vetting a Ghanaian police unit, whose members will then be trained by the DEA and for purposes of increasing Ghanaian counternarcotics interdiction capabilities and engaging in bilateral law enforcement operations with the DEA. In early 2009, a Colombian organized crime figure was extradited to the United States to face U.S. drug charges under the aegis of Ghanaian-DEA cooperation that involved use of DEA's extraterritorial authority, which facilitates U.S. prosecution of certain crimes committed overseas [39].

A modest International Military Education and Training (IMET) program supports military professionalism. Ghana was among the first recipients of peacekeeper training under the African Contingency Operations Training and Assistance program, a component of the State Department' Global Peace Operations Initiative (GPOI). In FY2010, GPOI is slated to continue to help train and equip Ghanaian forces deployed to international peace support operations, which has become a routine activity for Ghana. In FY2010, U.S. assistance will also "support Ghana in meeting its military pledges to the Economic Community of West African States Standby Force and international peacekeeping missions." The Department of Defense (DoD) has also provided Automated Identification System (AIS, a ship identifying system) equipment and fast patrol boats to Ghana. DoD has also engaged the Ghanaian military and civilian groups through its Africa Partnership Station, a DOD-sponsored effort to improve maritime security in West Africa that includes participation from U.S. civilian agencies and non-governmental actors. Ghana also acts as a base for periodic regional U.S military activities, such as crisis response actions or exercises. It also participates in the National Guard State Partnership Program, which links U.S. states (North Dakota in the case of Ghana) with partner nations in support of U.S security cooperation and broad bilateral goals.

Other Bilateral Assistance and Cooperation

A 171-member U.S. Peace Corps volunteer program pursues diverse projects, mostly in education, small business growth, environmental sustainability, and healthcare. After widespread flood damage in northern Ghana in September 2007, USAID's Office of U.S. Foreign Disaster Assistance provided $50,000 in emergency relief supplies to 5,000 recipients. The Treasury Department has also provided technical assistance to Ghana to help it issue Eurobonds.

Millennium Challenge Corporation

In August 2006, Ghana signed a $547 million, five-year MCC Compact. It supports investments in agriculture, production, business, and income growth (e.g., increasing exports and value-added business capacity, and improving irrigation and land tenure systems); in transportation; and programs to support rural government, social, and financial services. The MCC-Ghana partnership is intended to support the role of sound and institutionalized good governance and strong civil society engagement in sustainable development. Examples of current and recently completed achievements include the rehabilitation of 30 schools, and the on-going construction of 35 more, along with procurement to construct dozens more. In addition, Wide Area Network equipment aimed at automating and linking the payment systems of over 120 rural banks is currently being procured. Preparatory work on upgrading of the key N-1 Highway, which connects Ghana's major port to agricultural areas, is also on-going. Initial Farmer Based Organization (FBO) business plan development and crop productivity training has also been completed. Seven pineapple farms have also received pre-coolers and the design of a cold chain facility at Accra's Kotoka International Airport is being negotiated [40].

State Department and USAID Assistance Summary

Under the Administration's FY2010 budget request, core assistance to Ghana (exclusive of MCC, Peace Corps, and Defense Department assistance and food aid) would increase from the FY 2009 level of $115.4 million to $143.4 million.

Table 1. Bilateral State Department and USAID Assistance to Ghana, FY2008 to FY2010 ($ millions)

FY 2008 Actual		FY2009 Estimate	FY2010 Request
Development Assistance	25.4	59.5	71.1
Foreign Military Financing	0.3	0.3	0.5
Global Health and Child Survival-State	12.0	11.5	11.5
Global Health and Child Survival-USAID	35.1	38.5	59.0
International Military Education and Training	0.6	0.6	0.9
International Narcotics Control and Law Enforcement	0.5	0.5	0.5
Nonproliferation, Antiterrorism, Demining and Related Programs	0.1	-	-
Public Law 480 (Food Aid)	6.9	4.5	-
Total	80.9	115.4	143.4

Source: State Department, Congressional Budget Justification for Foreign Operations, FY2010.

The level of such assistance in FY2008 totaled $80.9 million. Food aid in FY2009 totaled $4.5 million, and an estimated $6.9 million in FY2008. The Administration did not request food aid specifically for Ghana in FY2010. Food aid may be allocated to Ghana in FY2010, however, and may rise in FY2009, as food aid is allocated from central accounts in response to need throughout the year.

REFERENCES

[1] White House, Statement by the Press Secretary on Upcoming Travel by the President, May 16, 2009 and Press Briefing by Press Secretary Robert Gibbs, June 22, 2009.

[2] White House, Statement by the Press Secretary on Upcoming Travel.

[3] White House, Readout of the President's call with President Mills of Ghana, Office of the Press Secretary, April 10, 2009. Mills won the run-off by garnering a 0.45% vote margin (40,586 votes of more than 9 million cast) over that of his opponent, New Patriotic Party (NPP) candidate Nana Akufo-Addo. Mills entered the run-off by coming in second in a preceding eight-candidate first round election, with 47. 06% votes cast, behind Akufo-Addo, who won a 47.55% vote share. Akufo-Addo's vote margin allowed him win the first round, but he failed to garner the 50% threshold needed to win the presidency outright, thus triggering the run-off. Electoral Commission of Ghana "Presidential (Runoff)," Election Results, January 3, 2009 and "2008 Results Summary - Final Results," online at http://ec.gov.gh/results; and; and BBC News, "Profile: Ghana President John Mills," January 3, 2009.

[4] White House, Readout of the President's call...; and U.S. Congress, Senate Committee on Foreign Relations, Confronting Drug Trafficking in West Africa, 111th Cong., 1st sess., June 23, 2009; and CRS report, forthcoming.

[5] This section, and all direct quotations within it, is drawn from a July 1, 2009 White House Press briefing on the President's trip to Russia, Italy, and Africa by Denis McDonough, Deputy National Security Advisor for Strategic Communications, Michael Froman, Deputy National Security Advisor for International Economic Affairs, Michelle Gavin, Special Assistant to the President and Senior Director for African Affairs, and Michael Mcfaul, Special Assistant to the President and Senior Director

for Russian and Eurasian Affairs, and in particular from comments made by Ms. Gavin.

[6] In a response to a reporter's question following the briefing, Ms. Gavin cited as examples of undemocratic changes of government in Africa coups d'état in Mauritania, Madagascar, and Guinea. She also cited as "problematic" elections in Nigeria, Kenya, Zimbabwe, and pointed to a further emerging challenge to democratic governance in Niger. Niger's President Mamadou Tandja has asserted a right to rule by emergency decree after failing to secure a constitutional change overturning term limits that would have allowed him to extend his tenure.

[7] See, for instance, U.S. Congress, Senate Committee on Foreign Relations, Confronting Drug Trafficking in West Africa, 111th Cong., 1st sess., June 23, 2009; H.R. 1410, Newborn, Child, and Mother Survival Act of 2009 (McCollum); H.Res. 550, Recognizing the "Day of the African Child" on June 16, 2009, devoted to the theme of child survival and to emphasize the importance of reducing maternal, newborn, and child deaths in Africa (Payne); and recent Dear Colleague letters on maternal health; and multiple bills and hearings focusing on food security in the 100th and 111th Congresses.

[8] According to the briefers, the first speech, in Prague, the Czech Republic, expressed President Obama's views on proliferation and the role of small states in the international system and in the context of U.S. national security goals. The second, in Cairo, Egypt, set out a vision for U.S. relations with communities in the Muslim world and associated issues faced jointly with those communities, e.g., terrorism, extremism, and lasting peace in the Middle East. A third speech, in Moscow, focused on U.S.-Russia relations and the role of great powers in the current century.

[9] Africa Confidential, "Lining up the Mills team," February 6, 2009; and Economist Intelligence Unit (EIU), Ghana Country Report, June 2009.

[10] NDC, A Better Ghana: Investing in People, Jobs and the Economy, 2008; and Parliament of Ghana, State of the Nation Address by His Excellency John Evans Mills, President of the Republic of Ghana, February 19, 2009.

[11] The manifesto states that the calls for "the NDC government" will establish s "Monitoring Unit that will watch and measure the implementation of the pledges and promise[s]" outlined in the document. All direct quotations in the following sections on Mills Administration policy are from the manifesto. NDC, A Better Ghana.

[12] See, among others, United Nations Integrated Regional Information Networks (IRIN), "Ghana: Critical issues in 7 December elections," December 4, 2008.

[13] Several leading contenders, dubbed the "monetocracy," reportedly funded expensive campaigns to court NPP delegates. Press reports raised questions over the funding sources of some NPP contenders. Africa Confidential, "Ghana: 'Who spends, wins'," November 30, 2007 and Africa Confidential, "Ghana, Race to the top," December 14, 2007, among others.

[14] The NPP has always fielded an ethnic Akan presidential and a vice-presidential candidate from the north since the reinstatement of multiparty politics in 1992, and is viewed as predominating in the Akan south and southeast. The NDC's traditional base of support, by contrast, is in the multi-ethnic, largely Islamic north and among Ewes in the south. Africa Confidential, "Ghana: 'Who spends...," inter alia.

[15] Coalition of Domestic Election Observers (CODEO), "Press Release (Close of Day)," December 7, 2008; EU Election Observation Mission, Republic of Ghana 2008, "Parliamentary and Presidential elections in Ghana conducted in an open, transparent and competitive environment," [press release], December 9, 2008; EU, European Union Election Observation Mission Ghana, "A Competitive Campaign and a High Degree of Transparency on Election Day Reflect Ghana's Democratic Culture," Presidential and Parliamentary Elections, 7 December 2008, Preliminary Statement, December 9, 2008; and Electoral Commission of Ghana, "AU observer team call on Minister," December 11, 2008, inter alia.

[16] Scott Stearns, "World Leaders Congratulate Ghana on Democratic Election," *Voice of America*," January 5, 2009.

[17] Ibid. Also see Ghana News Today via PeaceFMOnline.com, "5th Parliament to be Ushered in on Jan. 7th," January 3, 2009; Ghana News Agency (GNA) via Myjoyonline.Com, "Electoral offenders before court," January 6, 2009; and GNA via Myjoyonline.Com, "EC suspends Akwatia constituency parliamentary election," December 27, 2008.

[18] Kwasi Kpodo, "Ghana presidential hopefuls in last-ditch vote race," Reuters, December 31, 2008.

[19] Carter Center, "Carter Center Deploys Observers to Ghana's Brong-Ahafo Region to Observe Tain Constituency's Elections," December 31, 2008.

[20] Such an outcome was viewed as unlikely by press commentators, however, because in the first round, only 59% of Tain's voters had turned out. Of these voters, about 97% had reportedly split their ballots between the two leading candidates, with about 52% of these voters selecting Mills and about 48% choosing Akufo-Addo. CRS analysis and Xinhua, "Ghana presidential election results not declared for disputed votes in some areas," December 31, 2008, inter alia.

[21] Joy FM, "Ghanaian ruling party withdraws legal concerns relating to run-off polls," via OSC, January 2, 2009; Agence France Presse (AFP), "Violent protest over Ghana poll results," December 31, 2008; Kissy Agyeman, "Election 2008: Tensions Mount in Ghana as Electoral Commission Stalls Presidential Poll Announcement," Global Insight Daily Analysis, December 31, 2008; Media Foundation for West Africa, "Ghana: Opposition Party Supporters 'Allegedly' Assault Journalist in Accra," via OSC, January 3, 2009; Joy FM, "Defeated Ghanaian presidential candidate congratulates winner," via OSC, January 3, 2009; Ghanaian TV3, "Ghanaian ruling party presidential hopeful concedes defeat," via OSC January 3, 2009; and AFP, "Ghana: The Country Prepares for 2nd Alternate Power Handover in 10 Years," via OSC, January 4, 2009.

[22] Electoral Commission, "Latest News" and "Final Figures of the Presidential Run-off Elections," January 6, 2009.

[23] CIA 2008 World Factbook, among other sources.

[24] Interparliamentary Union data.

[25] Economist Intelligence Unit [EIU], Ghana Country Report, June 2009.

[26] Ibid; and past EIU data.

[27] See Oxfam America and the Integrated Social Development Center (ISODEC-Ghana), Ghana's Big Test: Oil's Challenge to Democratic Development, February 2009. See also commentary published by the Center for Global Development (CGD) Todd Moss, "Obama Right to Highlight Ghana's Success, But Will Oil Be the Spoiler?," CGD, July 6, 2009.

[28] West African Gas Pipeline Company (WAPCo), "First Gas Reaches Ghana," December 11, 2008; Kwasi Kpodo, "Ghana pipeline gets first Nigerian gas," Reuters via Thomson Financial News/Forbes, December 13, 2008; and Bank Information Center, "Update: West African Gas Pipeline comes online at last," December 18, 2008.

[29] Human Rights Watch, "Liberian President Must Be Arrested," June 4, 2003.

[30] State Department, Congressional Budget Justification for Foreign Operations [CBJ], FY20 10; and White House, Statement by the Press Secretary on Upcoming Travel.... In its FY2008 CBJ, for instance, the Bush Administration labeled Ghana "a key African partner" due to its role in promoting international security; its development of a "vibrant and stable" democracy; and its role as a key African market-oriented U.S. trading partner.

[31] CBJ, FY2010.

[32] The following bilateral assistance section draws from recent annual Congressional Budget Justifications (CBJ) for Foreign Operations and current and past USAID sectoral assistance fact sheets, among other sources. References to the Obama Administration's plans refer to and are drawn from the FY20 10 CBJ entry for Ghana. Unless otherwise noted, all direct quotations within the assistance section are from the FY 2010 CBJ.

[33] USAID, Governing Justly and Democratically, Activity Brief, May 2009; and FY 2008 and FY 2009 CBJs.

[34] Observers came from representatives of the 34 "independent, non-partisan civil society organizations" that make up the federation. See CODEO, "About CODEO," http://www.codeogh.org.

[35] A finding that was reflected by international observers; see, for instance, European Union Election Observation Mission, Ghana: Presidential and Parliamentary Elections 2008, Final Report, February 2009.

[36] USAID , Status of the Global Food Security Response in West Africa and Ghana, May 2009.

[37] See USAID, African Global Competitiveness Initiative (AGCI), http://www.usaid.gov/locations/subsaharan_africa/initiatives/agci.html

[38] Funding for these purposes comprised an average total of 1.4% of all State Department and USAID funding for Ghana between FY 2008 and projected FY 2010 funding.

[39] U.S. Congress, Senate Committee on Foreign Relations, Confronting Drug Trafficking in West Africa, 111th Cong., 1st sess., June 23, 2009.

[40] Ghana Compact documents online at http://www.mcc.gov; MCC, Ghana and MCC: An Innovative Partnership Delivering on America's Promise to Africa, June 5, 2009; and MCC, Compact Implementation Status Report, April- June 2009, inter alia.

INDEX

C

D

F

I

J

K

L

M

P

Q

R

S

T

U